FAITH IN HER WORDS

Over 100 women poets, spanning six centuries, make their appearance in this
new and lively selection—some for the first time.

There are no stereotypes here. The lives of the poets—revealed in the brief
biographies which precede each work—are as richly varied as the poems
themselves.

Here are poems which are witty, serious, reflective, humorous, sad, happy,
evocative. Some are by well-known writers—Emily Dickinson, Charlotte
Brontë, Alice Meynell, Christina Rossetti, Anne Bradstreet, Ruth Pitter—some
are by writers not known at all. Faith is central to the selection: some poems
search for faith, others rejoice in finding it. Many poets reflect with the eyes of
faith on their own world, work and relationships.

This is an anthology which rates high for sheer enjoyment.

VERONICA ZUNDEL is herself a poet and Christian feminist. She is the author
of a number of books, and compiler/presenter of anthologies such as The Lion
Book of Christian Classics and The Lion Book of Famous Prayers. She has
been assistant editor of Third Way magazine and contributed to several
volumes of poetry.

Faith in her words

SIX CENTURIES OF WOMEN'S POETRY

Compiled by Veronica Zundel

A LION PAPERBACK
Oxford · Batavia · Sydney

This collection, with editorial notes and biographies, copyright © 1991 Veronica Zundel
All poems by living poets and those who died less than fifty years ago are copyright and
are included by permission (see separate Acknowledgments).

Published by
Lion Publishing plc
Sandy Lane West, Oxford, England
ISBN 0 7459 1918 9
Lion Publishing Corporation
1705 Hubbard Avenue, Batavia, Illinois 60510, USA
ISBN 0 7459 1918 9
Albatross Books Pty Ltd
PO Box 320, Sutherland, NSW 2232, Australia
ISBN 0 7324 0283 2

First edition 1991
All rights reserved

British Library Cataloguing in Publication Data
Faith in her words: six centuries of women's poetry.
    1. Poetry in English. Women writers—Anthologies
    I. Zundel, Veronica
    821.00809287
    ISBN 0 7459 1918 9

Library of Congress Cataloging-in-Publication Data
Faith in her words: six centuries of women's poetry
    Compiled by Veronica Zundel. – 1st ed.
    ISBN 0 7459 1918 9
    1. English poetry–Women authors.
    2. American poetry–Women authors.
    3. Faith–Poetry. 4. Women–Poetry.
    I. Zundel Veronica.
    PR1117.P35 1991
    821.008'09287–dc20

Printed and bound in Great Britain
by Cox and Wyman Ltd, Reading

Contents

3 HER FELLOW-CREATURES

4 THE DAILY ROUND

5 HER PEN

6 HER LIFE'S SPAN

7 THE LAST ENEMY

PART TWO: HER NEIGHBOURS

8 THE OTHER HALF

9 LOVE'S JOY

13 FRIENDS AND FOES

14 JUSTICE

PART THREE: HER FAITH

15 GOD IN HER WORLD

16 GOD WITH HER

17 HER FAITH'S JOURNEY

18 PRAISE

Introduction

'I look everywhere for grandmothers and find none,' lamented Elizabeth Barrett Browning at the start of her poetic career.

Look into any general poetry anthology and you will find her complaint well justified. Only two or three major women poets appear—one of them usually Browning herself! All the other accomplished women poets of the ages are missing.

Yet, as this anthology clearly shows, women have always written poetry, often in spite of educational handicaps and active opposition. It is gaining recognition that has been hard. Many had the authorship of their works denied or attributed to men. Seventeenth-century poet Mary Masters, when told that some verses could not be hers because they were too good, pointed out 'in every line, distinguishing defects to prove them mine'! Other poets were hived off into 'children's poetry', even when they wrote for adults.

This is a grievous loss, particularly from a Christian viewpoint. If God has made two sexes to care for and develop the world, it is vital for both voices to be heard. And women poets of earlier centuries still speak to us with amazing freshness, and often with a wise and witty faith in God that can still stir the twentieth-century reader. (We can only guess how often the famous 'Anon' was a woman; but I have taken the liberty of assuming that she sometimes was.)

The pun in the title of this book is deliberate. For faith to be complete, it must be proclaimed 'in her words' as well as 'in his'. Most of the poets here (including all of the living ones) are Christians, and their faith illuminates their work. But truth as well as faith is a central Christian value. So I have also included some poets who struggled for faith, or were 'interested agnostics', and some whose faith was, in the words of the funeral service, 'known only to God', but who used the

11

Christian language of their society. They are here because I believe they tell some important truths about being a woman in this world, and because they tell them with laughter as well as tears. They express the title's other meaning: that in order to tell the truth about life, a woman poet must have 'faith in her words'.

Some readers may share my own difficulty with the use of 'men' to mean humanity. However, it would have been wrong to exclude poems which use this language simply because, at the time they were written, the issue was not under discussion.

PART ONE

Her World

This opening section launches us on a voyage of discovery, as poets explore the reality of being human and female. Rejoicing in the power of the senses, they yet feel the frustration of being confined to a human body; dreaming of escape from that body, they yet know that it is the only way they can experience the world—and God. As human beings, they know they are made in God's image; but as women, they are also made in the image of their society. Sometimes they long to solve the dilemma by seeking solitude, yet they know they cannot avoid the duties and responsibilities that society thrusts upon them.

So, with this contradictory mixture of joy and pain, of freedom and limitation, we follow the poet as she finds her feelings reflected in nature and in beloved places, as she delights in and suffers with her fellow creatures, as she strives to exercise her skills in rewarding work, as she tackles everyday tasks with humour and sometimes pleasure, as she expresses herself with her pen, as she faces her own maturing, ageing and mortality—and as in all these experiences she catches a glimpse of the God who created and calls her.

1 Herself

CHARLOTTE PERKINS GILMAN
1860–1935

Best known for her psychological chiller The Yellow Wallpaper, *Charlotte wrote other stories with a feminist slant. (In one, a woman wakes up to find she has become her husband!) Her book* Women and Economics *has been called 'the most influential book ever written by an American feminist'. A native of Connecticut, she lectured on ethics, economics and sociology and edited the magazine* The Forerunner. *Other books included* His Religion and Hers *and* In This Our World, *a collection of poems on women's issues.*

Birth

Lord, I am born!
I have built me a body
Whose ways are all open,
Whose currents run free,
From the life that is thine
Flowing ever within me,
To the life that is mine
Flowing outward through me.

I am clothed, and my raiment
Fits smooth the spirit,
The soul moves unhindered,
The body is free;
And the thought that my body
Falls short of expressing,
In texture and colour
Unfoldeth on me.

I am housed, O my Father,
My body is sheltered,
My spirit has room
'Twixt the whole world and me,
I am guarded with beauty and strength,
And within it
Is room for still union,
And birth floweth free.

And the union and birth
Of the house, ever growing,
Have built me a city,—
Have borne me a state—
Where I live manifold,
Many-voiced, many hearted,
Never dead, never weary,
And oh! never parted!
The life of the Human,
So subtle—so great!

Lord, I am born!
From inmost to outmost
The ways are all open,
The currents run free,
From thy voice in my soul
To my joy in the people—
I thank thee, O God,
For this body thou gavest,
Which enfoldeth the earth—
Is enfolded by thee!

EMILY DICKINSON
1830–1886

Neighbours in Amherst, Massachusetts, saw Emily as an eccentric spinster, flitting past them dressed all in white, like some strange moth. A lawyer's daughter, Emily was well educated. However, from her twenties, possibly after a frustrated love for a married preacher, she lived in almost total seclusion, leaving home only for long walks. During her life she allowed only two poems to appear in print; but after her death her sister Lavinia found nearly 2,000 in a box, written on envelopes, shopping lists, even sweet papers. Although she refused to join a church, many of her highly original, visionary poems show a mystical faith which is often Christian in its expression.

Bring me the sunset in a cup,
Reckon the morning's flagons up
And say how many dew,
Tell me how far the morning leaps,
Tell me what time the weaver sleeps
Who spun the breadths of blue.

Write me how many notes there be
In the new robin's extasy
Among astonished boughs,
How many trips the tortoise makes,
How many cups the bee partakes,
The debauchee of dews.

Also, who laid the rainbow's piers,
Also, who leads the docile spheres
By withes of supple blue?
Whose fingers string the stalactite,
Who counts the wampum[1] of the night
To see that none is due?
Who built this little alban house
And shut the windows down so close
My spirit cannot see?
Who'll let me out some gala day
With implements to fly away,
Passing pomposity?

---

[1] Wampum = string of beads used as a memory aid, and shell beads used as currency, by native Americans

ALICE MEYNELL
1847–1922

Born in London, Alice Thompson spent most of her childhood in Italy. Her father was a friend of Dickens and her sister, Lady Butler, a famous painter of battle pictures. Converted to Roman Catholicism at twenty-five, she married Wilfred Meynell, editor of a Catholic journal, when she was thirty. Together they befriended many great writers, taking the laudanum-addicted poet, Francis Thompson, into their simple but welcoming home. Alice published several volumes of essays but is best known for her accomplished, deeply Christian poetry.

To the body

Thou inmost, ultimate
Council of judgment, palace of decrees,
Where the high senses hold their spiritual state,
Sued by earth's embassies,
And sign, approve, accept, conceive, create;

Create—thy senses close
With the world's pleas. The random odours reach
Their sweetness in the place of thy repose,
Upon thy tongue the peach,
And in thy nostrils breathes the breathing rose.

To thee, secluded one,
The dark vibrations of the sightless skies,
The lovely inexplicit colours, run;
The light gropes for those eyes.
O thou august! thou dost command the sun.

Music, all dumb, hath trod
Into thine ear her one effectual way;
And fire and cold approach to gain thy nod,
Where thou call'st up the day,
Where thou awaitest the appeal of God.

CHRISTINA ROSSETTI
1830–94

Like many women poets, Christina led a very retired life, caring for her elderly mother. She twice rejected offers of marriage because of doctrinal differences, although she loved at least one of the men. Her faith was central to her life and to much of her poetry. Christina's earliest poems appeared in the magazine of the Pre-Raphaelite Brotherhood, of which her painter brother Dante Gabriel was a founder. She became famous with Goblin Market, *a vivid, strange fairy tale of two sisters, and subsequently published several more collections.*

Who shall deliver me?

God strengthen me to bear myself;
That heaviest weight of all to bear,
Inalienable weight of care.

All others are outside myself;
I lock my door and bar them out,
The turmoil, tedium, gad-about.

I lock my door upon myself,
And start self-purged upon the race
That all must run! Death runs apace.

If I could set aside myself,
And start with lightened heart upon
The road by all men overgone!

God harden me against myself,
This coward with pathetic voice
Who craves for ease, and rest, and joys:

Myself, arch-traitor to myself;
My hollowest friend, my deadliest foe,
My clog whatever road I go.

Yet One there is can curb myself,
Can roll the strangling load from me,
Break off the yoke and set me free.

ELIZABETH BARRETT BROWNING
1806–61

The love story of Elizabeth Barrett, a reclusive invalid, and Robert Browning, whose determination rescued her from the virtual imprisonment imposed by her domineering father, is well known from stage and screen versions. Less known is the fact that she was already well established as a poet (indeed in their lifetime she was the more famous) and that she held strong feminist views, expressed in the poetic novel Aurora Leigh. *The two poets settled in Italy, where Elizabeth improved in health and bore a son at over forty, as well as becoming a passionate supporter of the country's liberation movement.*

Education by an aunt
from Aurora Leigh

I danced the polka and Cellarius,
Spun glass, stuffed birds, and modelled flowers in wax,
Because she liked accomplishments in girls.
I read a score of books on womanhood
To prove, if women do not think at all,
They may teach thinking (to a maiden aunt
Or else the author),—books that boldly assert
Their right of comprehending husband's talk
When not too deep, and even of answering
With pretty 'may it please you,' or 'so it is,'—
Their rapid insight and fine aptitude,
Particular worth and general missionariness,
As long as they keep quiet by the fire
And never say 'no' when the world says 'ay',
For that is fatal—their angelic reach
Of virtue, chiefly used to sit and darn,
And fatten household sinners,—their, in brief,
Potential faculty in everything
Of abdicating power in it: she owned
She liked a woman to be womanly,
And English women, she thanked God and sighed
(Some people always sigh in thanking God)
Were models to the universe. And last
I learnt cross-stitch, because she did not like
To see me wear the night with empty hands
A-doing nothing...

         ...By the way,
The works of women are symbolical.
We sew, sew, prick our fingers, dull our sight,
Producing what? A pair of slippers, sir,
To put on when you're weary—or a stool
To stumble over and vex you...'curse that stool!'
Or else at best, a cushion, where you lean
And sleep, and dream of something we are not
But would be for your sake. Alas, alas!
This hurts most, this—that, after all, we are paid
The worth of our work, perhaps.

KATHERINE PHILIPS
1631–64

Katherine Fowler's earliest poems, written when she was fifteen, praised singleness but also depicted the ideal husband as 'some man of sense'. When her mother married Sir Richard Philips of Pembrokeshire, Katherine married his cousin James, thirty-eight years her senior. Their son, born after seven years, died at a few weeks old. Brought up a Presbyterian (she had read the whole Bible by four years old) Katherine later became an Anglican. Her Royalist politics saved her Parliamentarian husband's career at the Restoration. She formed a literary and religious circle, whose members took new names. Under hers, 'Orinda', she gained a great reputation, although the only collection published in her lifetime was an inaccurate 'pirated' version.

To one persuading a lady to a marriage

Forbear, bold youth; all's heaven here,
And what you do aver
To others courtship may appear,
'Tis sacrilege to her.
She is a public deity;
And were't not very odd
She should dispose herself to be
A petty household god?

First make the sun in private shine
And bid the world adieu,
That so he may his beams confine
In compliment to you:
But if of that you do despair,
Think how you do amiss
To strive to fix her beams which are
More bright and large than his.

VERONICA ZUNDEL
Born 1953

*Born in Coventry to Austrian parents, Veronica read English at Oxford, has taught
(very briefly!), worked for the Christian current affairs magazine* Third Way, *and
edited Bible reading notes. Published works include two anthologies of Christian
writing, a volume of her columns from* Christian Woman *magazine, and* Going Out,
*a book on dating. Among many committee jobs she has chaired the Christian feminist
group* Men, Women and God. *In 1989 she married Ed Sirett and now lives in North
London.*

*In this poem she plays with a favourite idea: that Eve's mistake was to undervalue
herself. What the tempter offered her—Godlikeness—she already had.*

Deception

In Eden's sun the woman basks,
she works, plays, loves as each day asks
and knows not she is God's mirror and sign;
till, curving elegant his tail,
the serpent (who is surely male)
insinuates a lack of the divine.

'To be like God' - a worthy goal
for any self-improving soul,
an offer she, or man, can scarce disdain.
Poor Eve! Why won't she realise
right now she's able, strong and wise
with nothing but the choice of good to gain?

Yet still the priests perpetuate
the lie that led to Eden's gate
and raised the fiery sword our bliss to bar:
still women make the same mistake
and bow to some religious snake
who tells us we are not the gods we are.

2 The World Around Her

CAROLINE SOUTHEY
1786–1854

Caroline Bowles grew up in Buckland Cottage, a small old Hampshire house surrounded by elms, with her retired naval captain father, her mother, maternal grandmother and great-grandmother. After her parents' death she survived on an annuity of £150 from an adopted stepbrother. Resolving to earn money by writing, she sent her narrative poem Ellen Fitzarthur *to the poet Robert Southey; it was eventually published anonymously. The widowed Southey continued to encourage her work, and in 1839 they married. However his growing senility and the hostility of her stepchildren made her miserable, and his death in 1843 was a relief. She returned to Buckland Cottage and wrote no more.*

The primrose

I saw it in my evening walk,
A little lonely flower!
Under a hollow bank it grew,
Deep in a mossy bower.

An oak's gnarled root, to roof the cave
With Gothic fretwork sprung,
Whence jewelled fern, and arum leaves,
And ivy garlands hung.

And from beneath came sparkling out
From a fall'n tree's old shell,
A little rill, that clipt about
The lady in her cell.

And there, methought, with bashful pride,
She seemed to sit and look
On her own maiden loveliness,
Pale imaged in the brook.

No other flower—no rival grew
Beside my pensive maid;
She dwelt alone, a cloistered nun,
In solitude and shade.

No sunbeam on that fairy well
Darted its dazzling light—
Only, methought, some clear, cold star
Might tremble there at night.

No ruffling wind could reach her there—
No eye, methought, but mine,
Or the young lamb's that came to drink,
Had spied her secret shrine.

And there was pleasantness to me
In such belief. Cold eyes
That slight dear Nature's lowliness,
Profane her mysteries.

Long time I looked and lingered there,
Absorbed in still delight—
My spirit drank deep quietness
In, with that quiet sight.

FELICIA HEMANS
1793–1835

'The stately homes of England, How beautiful they stand, To prove the upper classes Have still the upper hand.' Noel Coward's parody of one of Felicia Hemans' most popular poems is an ironical testimony to her fame. Brought up in Wales, the daughter of a Liverpool merchant, Felicia Browne was unhappily married to an Irish officer, Captain Hemans, who deserted her and her five sons. Her first volume of poems was published when she was fourteen and won praise from Shelley. She continued writing prolifically for adults and children, regarded as the greatest living woman poet and befriended by Wordsworth and Scott.

The homes of England

The stately Homes of England,
  How beautiful they stand!
Amidst their tall ancestral trees,
  O'er all the pleasant land.
The deer across their greensward bound,
  Through shade and sunny gleam,
And the swan glides past them with the sound
  Of some rejoicing stream.

The merry Homes of England!
  Around their hearths by night,
What gladsome looks of household love
  Meet in the ruddy light!
There woman's voice flows forth in song,
  Or childhood's tale is told,
Or lips move tunefully along
  Some glorious page of old.

The blessed Homes of England!
  How softly on their bowers
Is laid the holy quietness
  That breathes from Sabbath hours!
Solemn, yet sweet the church-bell's chime
  Floats through their woods at morn;
All other sounds, in that still time,
  Of breeze and leaf are born.

The Cottage Homes of England!
　By thousands on her plains,
They are smiling o'er the silvery brooks,
　And round the hamlet fanes.
Through glowing orchards forth they peep,
　Each from its nook of leaves,
And fearless there the lowly sleep,
　As the bird beneath their eaves.

The free, fair Homes of England!
　Long, long in hut and hall,
May hearts of native proof be reared
　To guard each hallowed wall!
And green for ever be the groves,
　And bright the flowery sod,
Where first the child's glad spirit loves
　Its country and its God!

CHARLOTTE BRONTË
1816–55

Haworth, the lonely moorland parsonage where the Brontës lived with their eccentric Irish father, is today a tourist centre. To the five girls and a boy who grew up there, it was a self-contained world from which they escaped by writing tales of a fantastical country. Unhappy at school, where the two eldest girls died, Charlotte and Emily were mostly educated at home with Anne. Charlotte worked as a governess, failed in an attempt to start a school, and taught for a year in Brussels, the scene of her novel Villette.

It was Charlotte's discovery of Emily's poems that spurred the three to publish a joint volume under the names of Currer, Ellis and Acton Bell (it sold two copies in its first year!). Later they all published novels, Charlotte's best loved being Jane Eyre. In 1854, after the deaths of Emily and Anne, Charlotte married her father's curate Arthur Nicholls, but died the following year in childbirth. This poem, often attributed to Emily, is probably by Charlotte.

Stanzas

Often rebuked, yet always back returning
To those first feelings that were born with me,
And leaving busy chase of wealth and learning
For idle dreams of things that cannot be:

Today, I will seek not the shadowy region;
Its unsustaining vastness waxes drear;
And visions rising, legion after legion,
Bring the unreal world too strangely near.

I'll walk, but not in old heroic traces,
And not in paths of high morality,
And not among the half-distinguished faces,
The clouded forms of long-past history.

I'll walk where my own nature would be leading:
It vexes me to choose another guide:
Where the gray flocks in ferny glens are feeding;
Where the wild wind blows on the mountain side.

What have those lonely mountains worth revealing?
More glory and more grief than I can tell:
The earth that wakes one human heart to feeling
Can centre both the worlds of Heaven and Hell.

DORA GREENWELL
1821–82

After the family home at Greenwell Ford, County Durham, was sold because of her father's debts, Dora had no settled home. She also struggled with poverty and ill health, but these circumstances only deepened her Christian faith. Her devotional work The Patience of Hope *impressed the poet and hymn writer John Greenleaf Whittier, and she published six volumes of poetry. Among her essays, 'Our Single Women' pleaded for greater work opportunities for educated women.*

A Scherzo (A shy person's wishes)

With the wasp at the innermost heart of a peach,
On a sunny wall out of tip-toe reach,
With the trout in the darkest summer pool,
With the fern-seed clinging behind its cool
Smooth frond, in the chink of an aged tree,
In the woodbine's horn with the drunken bee,
With the mouse in its nest in a furrow old,
With the chrysalis wrapt in its gauzy fold;
With things that are hidden, and safe, and bold,
With things that are timid, and shy, and free,
Wishing to be;
With the nut in its shell, with the seed in its pod,
With the corn as it sprouts in the kindly clod,
Far down where the secret of beauty shows
In the bulb of the tulip, before it blows;
With things that are rooted, and firm, and deep,
Quiet to lie, and dreamless to sleep;
With things that are chainless, and tameless, and proud,
With the fire in the jagged thunder-cloud,
With the wind in its sleep, with the wind in its waking,
With the drops that go to the rainbow's making,
Wishing to be with the light leaves shaking,
Or stones on some desolate highway breaking;
Far up on the hills, where no foot surprises
The dew as it falls, or the dust as it rises;
To be couched with the beast in its torrid lair,
Or drifting on ice with the polar bear,
With the weaver at work at his quiet loom;
Anywhere, anywhere, out of this room!

The sky is low

The sky is low, the clouds are mean,
A travelling flake of snow
Across a barn or through a rut
Debates if it will go.

A narrow wind complains all day
How someone treated him;
Nature, like us, is sometimes caught
Without her diadem.

Evening

She sweeps with many-coloured brooms,
And leaves the shreds behind;
Oh, housewife in the evening west,
Come back, and dust the pond!

You dropped a purple ravelling in,
You dropped an amber thread;
And now you've littered all the East
With duds of emerald!

And still she plies her spotted brooms,
And still the aprons fly,
Till brooms fade softly into stars—
And then I come away.

SARAH WILLIAMS
1841–68

Of Welsh origin, 'Sadie', the only child of a wealthy father, was educated at Queen's College, Harley Street, London. However, her strong social conscience led her to give her profits from writing ('God's money', as she called it) to the poor. She died after an operation for a terminal disease only months after her beloved father. Twilight Hours, a collection of her poems, was published posthumously.

Growth

A lonely rock uprose above the sea,
The coral insects fretting at its base;
And no man came unto its loneliness,
The very storm-birds shunned its evil case.
Only the ocean beat upon its breast,
Only the ocean gave it close embrace.

An island was upheaved towards the skies,
A central fire within its heart had burst;
The rock became a mountain, stern and strong,
Only the desolation shewed at first;
A stray bird dropped a seed that fructified,
No longer reigned the barrenness accursed.

A little world stood out among the seas,
With singing brooks and many a fragrant wood,
Where lovers heard again their story sweet,
And truth grew fair, more fully understood.
The tender flowers o'ergrew the chasms deep,
And God looked down, and saw that it was good.

LOUISE IMOGEN GUINEY
1861–1920

In her varied career Louise was first a journalist, then a postmistress in her native Massachusetts, then worked in the cataloguing department of the Boston Public Library, and finally emigrated to England to study in the Bodleian Library in Oxford. A Catholic, whose Irish lawyer father fought in the American Civil War, she was convent-educated and, this poem suggests, stirred by her Irish heritage. Her early volumes of poems won her literary friends, and her essays and letters were also collected and published.

In Leinster

I try to knead and spin, but my life is low the while.
O, I long to be alone and walk abroad a mile!
Yet if I walk alone, and think of naught at all,
Why from me that's young should the wild tears fall?

The shower-stricken earth, the earth-coloured streams,
They breathe on me awake and moan to me in dreams;
And yonder ivy fondling the broke castle-wall,
It pulls upon my heart till the wild tears fall.

The cabin door looks down a furze-lighted hill,
And far as Leighlin Cross the fields are green and still;
But once I hear the blackbird in Leighlin hedges call,
The foolishness is on me, and the wild tears fall.

DORA SIGERSON SHORTER
1866–1918

Dora's mother was a writer, her father a surgeon and Gaelic scholar. A native of Dublin, Dora was a close friend of Katharine Tynan and Louise Imogen Guiney. She was, like them, a Roman Catholic. On marrying journalist and critic Clement Shorter she moved to London, but at the 1916 Easter Rebellion she campaigned for the accused men and carved a memorial sculpture of the Irish patriots for Dublin cemetery. Her fourteen volumes of poems are largely narratives and ballads, many of them patriotic.

The gypsies' road

I shall go on the gypsies' road,
The road that has no ending;
For the sedge is brown on the lone lake side,
The wild geese eastward tending.

I shall go as the unfetter'd wave,
From shore to shore, forgetting
The grief that lies 'neath a roof-tree's shade,
The years that bring regretting.

No law shall dare my wandering stay,
No man my acres measure;
The world was made for the gypsies' feet,
The winding road for pleasure.

And I shall drift as the pale leaf stray'd,
Whither the wild wind listed,
I shall sleep in the dark of the hedge,
'Neath rose and thorn entwisted.

This was a call in the heart of the night,
A whispering dream's dear treasure:
'The world was made for the nomads' feet,
The winding road for pleasure.'

I stole at dawn from my roof-tree's shade,
And the cares that it did cover;
I flew to the heart of the fierce north wind,
As a maid will greet her lover.

But a thousand hands did draw me back
And bid me to their tending;
I may not go on the gypsies' road—
The road that has no ending.

KATHLEEN RAINE
Born 1908

Daughter of two London teachers, Kathleen spent childhood holidays with her grandmother in Northumberland. After her second marriage, to sociologist Charles Madge, was dissolved, Kathleen returned to the border country of her childhood. There she wrote her first volume of poems, inspired by nature and by the natural sciences she had studied at Cambridge. Her intense, mystical poetry has been compared to the work of Blake, the subject of much of her critical writing. This example echoes Blake in evoking the vividness of a child's experience.

Exile

Then, I had no doubt
That snowdrops, violets, all creatures, I myself
Were lovely, were loved, were love.
Look, they said,
And I had only to look deep into the heart,
Dark, deep into the violet, and there read,
Before I knew of any word for flower or love,
The flower, the love, the word.

They never wearied of telling their being; and I
Asked of the rose, only more rose, the violet
More violet; untouched by time
No flower withered or flame died,
But poised in its own eternity, until the looker moved
On to another flower, opening its entity.

ELIZABETH JENNINGS

Born 1926

'For me, poetry is always a search for order', says Elizabeth Jennings who has written since she was thirteen. A graduate of St Anne's College, Oxford, she has worked as a library assistant and as a publisher's reader, and has been a freelance writer for many years. She has travelled a great deal in Italy (painting is her second favourite art and the subject of many poems). 'My Roman Catholic religion and my poems are the most important things in my life,' she has said.

In a garden

When the gardener has gone this garden
Looks wistful and seems waiting an event.
It is so spruce, a metaphor of Eden
And even more so since the gardener went,

Quietly godlike, but, of course, he had
Not made me promise anything, and I
Had no one tempting me to make the bad
Choice. Yet still I felt lost and wonder why.

Even the beech tree from next door which shares
Its shadow with me, seemed a kind of threat.
Everything was too neat and someone cares

In the wrong way. I need not have stood long
Mocked by the smell of a mown lawn, and yet
I did. Sickness for Eden was so strong.

3 Her Fellow-Creatures

ANNA LAETITIA BARBAULD
1743–1825

Educated with the boys of her father's school in Leicestershire, Anna Aikin married a French dissenting minister, Rochemont Barbauld. It was her efforts and growing reputation as a writer which helped to make his school in Suffolk a success. They went on to run schools in North London, while she continued her writing career, producing devotional works for children and adults and editing classics of English literature.

from The mouse's petition to Doctor Priestley found in the trap where he had been confined all night

Oh! hear a pensive captive's prayer,
For liberty that sighs;
And never let thine heart be shut
Against the prisoner's cries.

For here forlorn and sad I sit,
Within the wiry grate;
And tremble at th'approaching morn,
Which brings impending fate.

If e'er thy breast with freedom glowed,
And spurned a tyrant's chain,
Let not thy strong oppressive force
A free-born mouse detain...

...If mind, as ancient sages taught,
A never-dying flame,
Still shifts through matter's varying forms,
In every form the same,

Beware, lest in the worm you crush
A brother's soul you find;
And tremble lest thy luckless hand
Dislodge a kindred mind.

Or, if this transient gleam of day
Be all of life we share,
Let pity plead within thy breast
That little all to spare.

So may thy hospitable board
With health and peace be crowned;
And every charm of heartfelt ease
Beneath thy roof be found.

So, when unseen destruction lurks,
Which mice like men may share,
May some kind angel clear thy path,
And break the hidden snare.

JOANNA BAILLIE
1762–1851

Joanna's father was a Scottish minister who became professor of Divinity at Glasgow; her uncles were the anatomists William and John Hunter, and her brother the famous physician Matthew Baillie. With this background she was well educated. She moved to London at an early age to lead a literary life in Hampstead. Her Plays on the Passions drew praise from Walter Scott. Other plays and dramatic poetry followed, and her popularity persisted throughout her long life.

from The kitten

...Backward coil'd, and crouching low,
With glaring eyeballs watch thy foe,
The housewife's spindle whirling round,
Or thread, or straw, that on the ground
Its shadows throws, by urchin sly
Held out to lure thy roving eye;
Then, onward stealing, fiercely spring
Upon the futile, faithless thing.
Now, wheeling round, with bootless skill,
Thy bo-peep tail provokes thee still,
As oft beyond thy curving side
Its jetty tip is seen to glide;
Till, from thy centre starting far,
Thou sidelong rear'st, with rump in air,
Erected stiff, and gait awry,
Like madam in her tantrums high...

...Then, beneath some urchin's hand
With modest pride thou tak'st thy stand,
While many a stroke of fondness glides
Along thy back and tabby sides.
Dilated swells thy glossy fur,
And loudly sings thy busy purr;
As, timing well the equal sound,
Thy clutching feet bepat the ground,
And all their harmless claws disclose
Like prickles of an early rose;
While softly from thy whisker'd cheek,
Thy half-clos'd eyes peer mild and meek.

*Self-willed and precocious, surgeon's daughter Jane Welsh insisted on a good
education. Sent to Haddington School to learn Latin, she fell in love with master
Edward Irving. For his sake she refused all suitors. However, he got engaged to another
woman, who would not part with him—though he still visited Jane. Irving introduced
her to Thomas Carlyle, who, after five years, persuaded her to marry him. It was a
lonely marriage, with Carlyle engrossed in his work, and with little money. But after a
move from Edinburgh to London Jane made new friends and Carlyle's growing success
eased their finances. Knocked down by a cab in 1863, Jane never fully recovered. In
1866 she went for a drive, stopped to pick up a stray dog, and was found dead with the
dog in her lap.*

To a swallow building under our eaves

Thou too hast travelled, little fluttering thing—
Hast seen the world, and now thy weary wing
   Thou too must rest.
But much, my little bird, couldst thou but tell,
I'd give to know why here thou lik'st so well
   To build thy nest.

For thou hast passed fair places in thy flight;
A world lay all beneath thee where to light;
   And, strange thy taste,
Of all the varied scenes that met thine eye—
Of all the spots for building 'neath the sky—
   To choose this waste.

Did fortune try thee? was thy little purse
Perchance run low, and thou afraid of worse,
   Felt here secure?
Oh no! thou need'st not gold, thou happy one!
Thou know'st it not. Of all God's creatures, man
   Alone is poor!

What was it, then? some mystic turn of thought,
Caught under German eaves, and hither brought,
   Marring thine eye
For the world's loveliness, till thou art grown
A sober thing that dost but mope and moan
   Not knowing why?

Nay, if thy mind be sound, I need not ask,
Since here I see thee working at thy task
   With wing and beak.
A well-laid scheme doth that small head contain,
At which thou work'st, brave bird, with might and main,
   Nor more need'st seek.

In truth, I rather take it thou hast got
By instinct wise much sense about thy lot,
   And hast small care
Whether an Eden or a desert be
Thy home so thou remain'st alive, and free
   To skim the air.

God speed thee, pretty bird, may thy small nest
With little ones all in good time be blest.
   I love thee much;
For well thou managest that life of thine,
While I! O ask not what I do with mine!
   Would I were such!

CHRISTINA ROSSETTI
1830–94

A frog's fate

Contemptuous of his home beyond
The village and the village-pond,
A large-souled Frog who spurned each byeway
Hopped along the imperial highway.

Nor grunting pig nor barking dog
Could disconcert so great a Frog.
The morning dew was lingering yet,
His sides to cool, his tongue to wet:
The night-dew, when the night should come,
A travelled Frog would send him home.

Not so, alas! The wayside grass
Sees him no more: not so, alas!
A broad-wheeled wagon unawares
Ran him down, his joys, his cares.
From dying choke one feeble croak
The Frog's perpetual silence broke:-
'Ye buoyant Frogs, ye great and small,
Even I am mortal after all!
My road to fame turns out a wry way;
I perish on the hideous highway;
Oh for my old familiar byeway!'

The choking Frog sobbed and was gone;
The Waggoner strode whistling on.
Unconscious of the carnage done,
Whistling that Waggoner strode on—
Whistling (it may have happened so)
'A froggy would a-wooing go.'
A hypothetic frog trolled he,
Obtuse to a reality.

O rich and poor, O great and small,
Such oversights beset us all.
The mangled Frog abides incog,
The uninteresting actual frog:
The hypothetic frog alone
Is the one frog we dwell upon.

IRINA RATUSHINSKAYA
Born 1954

At only nine Irina rebelled against Soviet philosophy, concluding that if her teachers tried so hard to disprove God, he must exist! To avoid the conflicts which studying literature would arouse, she studied natural science and took a teaching post. But she never stopped writing poetry. In 1979 she married the human rights activist Igor Gerashchenko, and became involved in protests which cost both of them their jobs. In 1983 she was sentenced to seven years' hard labour for 'the manufacture and dissemination of poems'. During her imprisonment her poems were smuggled to the West, and following worldwide protest she was released in October 1986. She now lives in Britain.

The spider-mathematician
translated by David McDuff

The spider-mathematician (hard to imagine a sorrier creature!)
Keeps trying to count his thin little legs.
But sensibly he doesn't believe the tiny number he ends up with
And angrily mutters: 'The damned thing won't work out again!'
He has woven diagrams, assiduously measured the angles,
He solves the problem of which is the wolf and which the goat
With a cabbage leaf, but doesn't believe the result and once again
Rustles hopelessly and sighs: 'I know the answer, but how to prove it?'
O potty genius, crucified on coordinates,
Eccentric Pythagoras, half-witted prison prophet!
Wait before you creep away: I believe your results!
Spread out your diagram, and count the days of my sentence, please.

BARBARA DICKINSON
Born 1922

*'The poems come of their own accord, often at inconvenient moments,' says Barbara—
she was once doing a crossword puzzle on a train when 'a poem took over'. She spent
her whole working life as a civil servant, apart from six months in industry after the
war, 'where I learnt what Disraeli meant by "two nations"'. She has won many prizes,
including the Julia Cairns Award of the Society of Women Writers. She helps edit
various poetry magazines and has published two collections,* Gaze an Eagle Blind
and Merry Days of Desolation.

Go to the ant

I have always considered
the grasshopper
to be the finer fellow
He did not scrape and hoard
worldly possessions
He would not have turned away
a friend hungry
He had more fun
in one fiddle foot
than the ant in his
whole diligent body
Gladly the grasshopper
glorified God by the
sensuous enjoyment
of each irretrievable moment
while the ant
grieved his yesterdays
and grumbled each tomorrow

IS THERE A LIFE BEFORE DEATH?

wrote the grasshopper
on the lavatory wall
and added

NOT FOR ANTS

4 The Daily Round

MARY LAMB
1765–1847

On the death of his employer, Mary Lamb's father was left in some poverty to support his wife and children, Mary and Charles (their elder brother John, though better off, gave them little support). Mary supported herself by needlework. She cared for her invalid mother but in 1796, in a fit of mental instability, killed her with a table knife. Charles, ten years younger, devoted himself to caring for Mary between her occasional periods in asylums. They wrote their famous Tales from Shakespeare *together, as well as poems and stories for children. Charles gained fame as an essayist; Mary was less known, but her contribution to their joint volumes of poetry is substantial, especially in 'celebrations of the everyday' like this one.*

Breakfast

A dinner-party, coffee, tea,
Sandwich, or supper, all may be
In their way pleasant. But to me
Not one of these deserves the praise
That welcomer of new-born days,
A breakfast, merits; ever giving
Cheerful notice we are living
Another day refreshed by sleep,
When its festival we keep.
Now, although I would not slight
Those kindly words we use, 'Good-night',
Yet parting words are words of sorrow,
And may not vie with sweet 'Good-morrow',
With which again our friends we greet,
When in the breakfast-room we meet,
At the social table round,
Listening to the lively sound
Of those notes which never tire,
Of urn, or kettle on the fire.

Sleepy Robert never hears
Or urn or kettle; he appears
When all have finished, one by one
Dropping off, and breakfast done.
Yet has he too his own pleasure—

His breakfast hour's his hour of leisure;
And, left alone, he reads or muses,
Or else in idle mood he uses
To sit and watch the venturous fly,
Where the sugar's piled high,
Clambering o'er the lumps so white,
Rocky cliffs of sweet delight.

TRADITIONAL CELTIC

The poetry of the Gaelic-speaking people of Scotland, their authors lost in history, has been handed down orally for many generations, often by the women. Many were collected and translated by Alexander Carmichael in his 1899 Carmina Gadelica. Songs of fire-kindling, milking, weaving and other tasks of the farming household are likely to have been composed by women, since they did the bulk of this work.

Loom blessing

Thrums nor odds of thread
My hand never kept, nor shall keep,

Every colour in the bow of the shower
Has gone through my fingers beneath the cross,

White and black, red and madder,
Green, dark grey, and scarlet,

Blue, and roan, and colour of the sheep,
And never a particle of cloth was wanting.

I beseech calm Bride the generous,
I beseech mild Mary the loving,
I beseech Christ Jesu the humane,
That I may not die without them,
    That I may not die without them.

Milking croon

Bless, O God, my little cow,
Bless, O God, my desire;
Bless Thou my partnership
And the milking of my hands, O God.

Bless, O God, each teat,
Bless, O God, each finger;
Bless Thou each drop
That goes into my pitcher, O God!

MARY COLLIER
?1690–1762

Born to 'poor but honest' parents in Midhurst, Sussex, who taught her to read but could not afford to send her to school, Mary moved after her father's death to Petersfield, Hampshire 'where my chief employment was washing, brewing and such labour, still devoting what leisure time I had to books'. It was in reply to a poem by Stephen Duck on the 'idleness of rural women' that she wrote this indignant defence, which was published at her own expense. In later years she ran a farm, retiring at seventy to 'a garret, the poor poet's fate'.

from The woman's labour

When bright Orion glitters in the skies
In winter nights, then early we must rise;
The weather ne'er so bad, wind, rain or snow,
Our work appointed, we must rise and go,
While you on easy beds may lie and sleep,
Till light does through your chamber windows peep.
When to the house we come where we should go,
How to get in, alas! we do not know:
The maid quite tired with work the day before,
O'ercome with sleep; we standing at the door,
Oppressed with cold, and often call in vain,
Ere to our work we can admittance gain.
But when from wind and weather we get in,
Briskly with courage we our work begin;
Heaps of fine linen we before us view,
Where on to lay our strength and patience too;
Cambrics and muslins, which our ladies wear,
Laces and edgings, costly, fine and rare,
Which must be washed with utmost skill and care;
With holland shirts, ruffles and fringes too,
Fashions which our forefathers never knew.
For several hours here we work and slave,
Before we can one glimpse of daylight have;
We labour hard before the morning's past,
Because we fear the time runs on too fast.

At length bright Sol illuminates the skies,
And summons drowsy mortals to arise;
Then comes our mistress to us without fail,
And in her hand, perhaps, a mug of ale

To cheer our hearts, and also to inform
Herself what work is done that very morn;
Lays her commands upon us, that we mind
Her linen well, nor leave the dirt behind.
Not this alone, but also to take care
We don't her cambrics nor her ruffles tear;
And these most strictly does of us require,
To save her soap and sparing be of fire;
Tells us her charge is great, nay furthermore,
Her clothes are fewer than the time before.
Now we drive on, resolved our strength to try,
And what we can we do most willingly;
Until with heat and work, 'tis often known,
Not only sweat but blood runs trickling down
Our wrists and fingers: still our work demands
The constant action of our labouring hands.

The aristocratic little girl who once ran away with her brother to 'die as martyrs in Morocco' grew up to reform the then lackadaisical Carmelite order. Though her dramatic visions of an angel piercing her heart with a sword made some think her neurotic, she was in fact a thoroughly practical woman. Teresa joined in her nuns' manual work, discouraged religious excess and prayed for deliverance from 'silly devotions and sour-faced saints'. This chant was used when the nuns feared an invasion of parasites in their new habits of coarse frieze.

Hymn for the nuns' new habits
translated by E. Allison Peers

Since Thou giv'st us, King of Heaven,
New clothes like these,
Do Thou keep all nasty creatures
Out of this frieze.

Daughters, you've the cross upon you;
Have courage too.
Since salvation He has won you,
He'll bring you through.
He'll direct you, He'll defend you,
If Him you please.
Do Thou keep all nasty creatures
Out of this frieze.

Drive away whate'er molests you
With fervent prayer;
Nothing else so surely tests you
If love is there.
God will help you if within you
Firm trust He sees.
Do Thou keep all nasty creatures
Out of this frieze.

Since you came prepar'd to die here
Be not dismay'd;
Ne'er must things that creep and fly here
Make you afraid.
Help your God will always send you
'Gainst plagues like these.
Do Thou keep all nasty creatures
Out of this frieze.

MARY JONES
Died 1778

Much admired by fellow poets of her day—Alexander Pope 'borrowed' some of her lines, the sincerest form of flattery!—Mary came from a middle-class Oxford family. She was well educated, learning French and Italian, from which she translated some works. She lived in Oxford with her brother, the Rev. Oliver Jones, but often visited London friends, one of whom was maid of honour to Princess Caroline. She concealed her writing from friends but was persuaded to publish some verses, and appears in the contemporary collection Poems by Eminent Ladies.

Soliloquy upon an empty purse

Alas! my Purse! how lean and low!
My silken Purse! what art thou now!
Once I beheld—but stocks will fall—
When both thy ends had wherewithal.
When I within thy slender fence
My fortune plac'd, and confidence;
My poet's fortune! - not immense:
Yet, mixt with keys, and coins among,
Chinkt to the melody of song.

   Canst thou forget, when, high in air,
I saw thee, fluttering at a fair?
And took thee, destin'd to be sold,
My lawful Purse to have and hold?
Yet us'd so oft to disembogue,
No prudence could thy fate prorogue.
Like wax thy silver melted down,
Touch but the brass, and lo! 'twas gone:
And gold would never with thee stay,
For gold had wings, and flew away.

   Alas, my Purse! yet still be proud,
For see the virtues round thee crowd!
See, in the room of paltry wealth,
Calm temperance rise, the nurse of health;
And self-denial, slim and spare,
And fortitude, with look severe;
And abstinence, to leanness prone,
And patience worn to skin and bone.
Prudence and foresight on thee wait,
And poverty lies here in state!
Hopeless their spirits to recruit,

For ev'ry virtue is a mute.
    Well then, my Purse, thy sabbaths keep;
Now thou art empty, I shall sleep.
No silver sounds shall thee molest,
Nor golden dreams disturb my breast.
Safe shall I walk the streets along,
Amidst temptations thick and strong...
...Beholding all with equal eye,
Nor mov'd at—'Madam, what d'ye buy?'

    Away, far hence each worldly care!
Nor dun, nor pick-purse shalt thou fear,
Nor flatt'rer base annoy my ear.
Snug shalt thou travel through the mob,
For who a poet's purse will rob?
And softly sweet in garret high
Will I thy virtues magnify;
Out-soaring flatt'rers stinking breath,
And gently rhyming rats to death.

ANNE STEELE
Died ?1779

The daughter of a Nonconformist preacher in Hampshire, Anne Steele wrote a metrical version of the psalms and many hymns which were popular in their day, though none survive in today's hymn books. This poem is of historical interest, coming from an age where pocket watches for women were still something of a novelty.

To my watch

Little monitor, by thee
Let me learn what I should be;
Learn the round of life to fill,
Useful and progressive still.
Thou can'st gentle hints impart
How to regulate the heart;
When I wind thee up at night,
Mark each fault and set thee right,
Let me search my bosom too,
And my daily thoughts review;
Mark the movements of my mind,
Nor be easy till I find
Latent errors brought to view,
Till all be regular and true.

ALICE DUNBAR NELSON
1875–1935

A native of New Orleans, Alice Moore was well educated, and for most of her life she was a teacher. Her husband Paul Dunbar was the first black poet to achieve wide literary acceptance in America. Together they collected great black literature to be performed on stage. This poem was Alice's contribution, one of the few she wrote.

I sit and sew

I sit and sew—a useless task it seems,
My hands grown tired, my head weighed down with dreams—
The panoply of war, the material tread of men,
Grim-faced, stern-eyed, gazing beyond the ken
Of lesser souls, whose eyes have not seen Death,
Nor learned to hold their lives but as a breath—
But—I must sit and sew.

I sit and sew—my heart aches with desire—
That pageant terrible, that fiercely pawing fire
On wasted fields, and writhing grotesque things
Once men. My soul in pity flings
Appealing cries, yearning only to go
There in that holocaust of hell, those fields of woe—
But—I must sit and sew.

The little useless seam, the idle patch;
Why dream I here beneath my homely thatch,
When there they lie in sodden mud and rain,
Pitifully calling me, the quick ones and the slain!
You need me, Christ! It is no roseate dream
That beckons me—this pretty futile seam,
It stifles me—God, must I sit and sew?

EDITH NESBIT
1858–1924

Best loved for her delightful children's novels—among them The Treasure Seekers,
Five Children and It, The Railway Children—*Edith first appeared in print with a
poem. Educated in France, Germany and Brighton, she married Hubert Bland and,
after his death, engineer Thomas Tucker. Having strong socialist sympathies, she
named one of her sons Fabian, after the Fabian Society! In 1915 her work gained her a
Civil List pension.*

The things that matter

Now that I've nearly done my days,
And grown too stiff to sweep or sew,
I sit and think, till I'm amaze,
About what lots of things I know:
Things as I've found out one by one—
And when I'm fast down in the clay,
My knowing things and how they're done
Will all be lost and thrown away.

There's things, I know, as won't be lost,
Things as folks write and talk about:
The way to keep your roots from frost,
And how to get your ink spots out.
What medicine's good for sores and sprains,
What way to salt your butter down,
What charms will cure your different pains,
And what will bright your faded gown.

But more important things than these,
They can't be written in a book:
How fast to boil your greens and peas,
And how good bacon ought to look;
The feel of real good wearing stuff,
The kind of apple as will keep,
The look of bread that's rose enough,
And how to get a child asleep.

Whether the jam is fit to pot,
Whether the milk is going to turn,
Whether a hen will lay or not,
Is things as some folks never learn.
I know what weather by the sky,

I know what herbs grow in what lane;
And if sick men are going to die,
Or if they'll get about again.

Young wives come in, a-smiling, grave,
With secrets that they long to tell:
I know what sort of times they'll have,
And if they'll have a boy or gell.
And if a lad is ill to bind,
Or some young maid is hard to lead,
I know when you should speak 'em kind,
And when it's scolding as they need.

I used to know where birds ud set,
And likely spots for trout or hare,
And God may want me to forget
The way to set a line or snare;
But not the way to truss a chick,
To fry a fish, or baste a roast,
Nor how to tell, when folks are sick,
What kind of herbs will ease them most!

Forgetting seems such silly waste!
I know so many little things,
And now the Angels will make haste
To dust it all away with wings!
O God, you made me like to know,
You kept the things straight in my head,
Please God, if you can make it so,
Let me know something when I'm dead.

GWEN CLEAR

Early twentieth century

Despite the warm, witty and often profoundly Christian poetry found in her 1927
collection The Eldest Sister, *Gwen Clear seems to have vanished from literary history*
since. Not even her dates are listed in biographical reference works. In 1949 she wrote
a biography of the bookseller W.H.Smith. No other works are recorded.

The goodwife relents

My dear, I cannot tell
How it could come about
That we, who loved so well,
Should turn to falling out,
But since the spring is come
With running sap and leaves
Strong-shooting from the boughs,
And swallows in the eaves,
Since spring is come with rain
To green and hidden ditches,
We'll mend the purse of love
With quick and purposed stitches.
Haste—April flies—
The winter bridge is down;
You must to the market
And I must to the town.

For you must buy a horse,
And a cow, and a cart,
And I must buy a quartern loaf
And half a gooseberry tart.
You must buy a rake
And a shovel and a hoe,
And I must buy some flowering chintz
And a bale of calico.
O and a rug with fringes
To spread along the floor,
And half an ounce of aniseed
And a handle for the door.
The gate is off its hinges,
The thatch is working down,
You must to the market,
And I must to the town.

My dear, I cannot tell
How it would come about
That we, who loved so well,
Should turn to falling out,
But since the spring is come
We'll have no more denying
Of one who hid his wings
Yet secretly was flying.
Since spring is come with rain,
And with the leaves of clover
And lovelier celandine
The fields are sprinkled over,
Haste—April flies—
I bid you Love, be merry,
Where singing hangs the thrush
Beneath the flowering cherry.

U. A. FANTHORPE
Born 1929

'I've been in love with the English language since I first learned to speak.' After gaining an Oxford degree and working as a teacher at Cheltenham Ladies College, for which she 'had no temperament', Ursula Fanthorpe became a receptionist at a small hospital. 'Poetry struck during my first month behind the desk...I think...because of the rage and frustration I felt.' She lives in Gloucestershire, has had several collections published and has been an Arts Council Fellow in Writing.

The list

Flawlessly typed, and spaced
At the proper intervals,
Serene and lordly, they pace
Along tomorrow's list
Like giftbearers on a frieze.

In tranquil order, arrayed
With the basic human equipment—
A name, a time, a number—
They advance on the future.

Not more harmonious who pace
Holding a hawk, a fish, a jar
(The customary offerings)
Along the valley of the kings.

Tomorrow these names will turn nasty,
Senile, pregnant, late,
Handicapped, handcuffed, unhandy,
Muddled, moribund, mute,

Be stained by living. But here,
Orderly, equal, right,
On the edge of tomorrow, they pause
Like giftbearers on a frieze

With the proper offering,
A time, a number, a home.
I am the artist, the typist;
I did my best for them.

5 Her Pen

ANNE FINCH, COUNTESS OF WINCHILSEA
1661–1720

Daughter of an aristocratic Hampshire family, Anne became maid of honour to Mary, wife of King James II. To marry Colonel Heneage Finch at eighteen, she added five years to her age in the parish register! With the fall of James II, she and her husband, now a member of Parliament, were out of favour; but he later succeeded to his nephew's title as Earl of Winchilsea. A staunch Anglican and Tory, Anne moved in literary circles, corresponded with the poet Pope and had her collected poems published in 1713. The most popular in her lifetime was 'The Spleen', a long poem on her recurrent depression.

The apology

'Tis true, I write; and tell me by what rule
I am alone forbid to play the fool,
To follow through the groves a wandering muse
And feigned ideas for my pleasures choose?
Why should it in my pen be thought a fault,
While Myra paints her face, to paint a thought?
Whilst Lamia to the manly bumper[1] flies,
And borrowed spirits sparkle in her eyes,
Why should it be in me a thing so vain
To heat with poetry my colder brain?

But I write ill, and therefore should forbear.
Does Flavia cease now at her fortieth year
In every place to let that face be seen
Which all the town rejected at fifteen?
Each woman has her weakness; mine indeed
Is still to write, though hopeless to succeed.
Nor to the men is this so easy found;
Even in most works with which the wits abound
(So weak are all since our first breach with Heaven)
There's less to be applauded than forgiven.

[1] Bumper = a drinking glass filled to the brim

MARY LEAPOR

1722–46

As a child Mary loved reading, though there were only sixteen books in her gardener father's Northamptonshire home. She probably worked as a kitchen maid; but her poems under the name of 'Mira' were noticed by 'persons of rank' including actor David Garrick, who planned to publish them. Sadly, she died of smallpox before their appearance. Her work, which was admired by William Cowper, turns a satirical eye on everything including her own plainness.

Upon her play being returned to her stained with claret

Welcome, dear wanderer, once more!
Thrice welcome to thy native cell!
Within this peaceful humble door
Let thou and I contented dwell.

But say, O whither hast thou ranged?
Why dost thou blush a crimson hue?
Thy fair complexion's greatly changed;
Why, I can scarce believe it's you.

Then tell, my son, O tell me where
Didst thou contract this sottish dye?
You kept ill company, I fear,
When distant from your parent's eye.

Was it for this, O graceless child!
Was it for this you learned to spell?
Thy face and credit both are spoiled:
Go drown thyself in yonder well.

I wonder how thy time was spent:
No news (alas!) hast thou to bring?
Hast thou not climbed the Monument?
Nor seen the lions, nor the King?

But now I'll keep you here secure:
No more you view the smoky sky;
The court was never made (I'm sure)
For idiots, like thee and I.

*'She never held herself up as a writer; when she resorted to her pen, it was either to
amuse a leisure hour, to gratify an absent friend, or for the sublimer purpose of pouring
out her heart in praise and thanksgiving to God,' remembered Mary's niece. A
Northamptonshire vicar's daughter, Mary Cumberland went to Ireland with her
parents and there married Archdeacon Alcock. After his death she lived in Bath,
supported several nieces and published occasional verses including a response to the
new craze of ballooning. Always frail, she died on a journey to York. Her poems were
published posthumously.*

from A receipt for writing a novel

...Of love take first a due proportion—
It serves to keep the heart in motion:
Of jealousy a powerful zest,
Of all tormenting passions best;
Of horror mix a copious share,
And duels you must never spare;
Hysteric fits at least a score,
Or, if you find occasion, more;
But fainting-fits you need not measure,
The fair ones have them at their pleasure;
Of sighs and groans take no account,
But throw them in to vast amount;
A frantic fever you may add,
Most authors make their lovers mad;
Rack well your hero's nerves and heart,
And let your heroine take her part;
Her fine blue eyes were made to weep,
Nor should she ever taste of sleep;
Ply her with terrors day and night,
And keep her always in a fright...

...A cruel father some prepare
To drag her by her flaxen hair;
Some raise a storm, and some a ghost,
Take either, which may please you most.
But this you must with care observe,
That when you've wound up every nerve
With expectation, hope and fear,
Hero and heroine must disappear.

Some fill one book, some two without 'em
And ne'er concern their heads about 'em:
This greatly rests the writer's brain,
For any story, that gives pain,
You now throw in—no matter what,
However foreign to the plot;
So it but serves to swell the book,
You foist it in with desperate hook—
A masquerade, a murdered peer,
His throat just cut from ear to ear—
A rake turned hermit—a fond maid
Run mad, by some false loon betrayed—
These stores supply the female pen,
Which writes them o'er and o'er again,
And readers likewise may be found
To circulate them round and round.

Now, at your fable's close, devise
Some grand event to give surprise—
Suppose your hero knows no mother—
Suppose he proves the heroine's brother—
This at one stroke dissolves each tie,
Far as from east to west they fly:
At length, when every woe's expended,
And your last volume's nearly ended,
Clear the mistake, and introduce
Some tattling nurse to cut the noose;
The spell is broke—again they meet
Expiring at each other's feet;
Their friends lie breathless on the floor—
You drop your pen; you can no more—
And ere your reader can recover,
They're married—and your history's over.

ALICE MEYNELL
1847–1922

To any poet

Thou who singest through the earth
All the earth's wild creatures fly thee;
Everywhere thou marrest mirth,—
    Dumbly they defy thee;
There is something they deny thee.

Pines thy fallen nature ever
For the unfallen Nature sweet.
But she shuns thy long endeavour,
    Though her flowers and wheat
Throng and press thy pausing feet.

Though thou tame a bird to love thee,
Press thy face to grass and flowers,
All these things reserve above thee
    Secrets in the bowers,
Secrets in the sun and showers.

Sing thy sorrow, sing thy gladness,
In thy songs must wind and tree
Bear the fictions of thy sadness,
    Thy humanity.
For their truth is not for thee.

Wait, and many a secret nest,
Many a hoarded winter-store
Will be hidden on thy breast.
    Things thou longest for
Will not fear or shun thee more.

Thou shalt intimately lie
In the roots of flowers that thrust
Upwards from thee to the sky,
    With no more distrust
When they blossom from thy dust.

Silent labours of the rain
Shall be near thee, reconciled;
Little lives of leaves and grain,
    All things shy and wild,
Tell thee secrets, quiet child.

Earth, set free from thy fair fancies
And the art thou shalt resign,
Will bring forth her rue and pansies
    Unto more divine
Thoughts than any thoughts of thine.

Nought will fear thee, humbled creature.
There will lie thy mortal burden
Pressed unto the heart of Nature,
    Songless in a garden,
With a long embrace of pardon.

Then the truth all creatures tell,
And His will Whom thou entreatest,
Shall absorb thee; there shall dwell
    Silence, the completest
Of thy poems, last, and sweetest.

STEVIE SMITH
1902–1971

From the age of three to her death, Florence Margaret Smith (Stevie was a teenage nickname) lived quietly in the London suburb of Palmers Green (affectionately parodied as 'Bottle Green' in her autobiographical Novel on Yellow Paper*) with her mother and later her aunt, whom she called the 'Lion of Hull'. She spent her whole working life as secretary to a magazine publisher. Her eight collections of quirky, individual poems earned her the Queen's Medal for Poetry in 1969. Though she lost her childhood faith, she retained an ambivalent but strong fascination with the Church of England.*

'What is she writing? Perhaps it will be good'

'What is she writing? Perhaps it will be good,'
The young girl laughs: 'I am in love.'
But the older girl is serious: 'Not now, perhaps later.'
Still the young girl teases: 'What's the matter?
To lose everything! A waste of time!'
But now the older one is quite silent,
Writing, writing, and perhaps it will be good.
Really neither girl is a fool.

6 Her Life's Span

ANONYMOUS, FOURTEENTH CENTURY
Translated by the editor

*At a time of more superstition than medical knowledge, with civil disturbances and the
Black Death sweeping Europe, the precariousness and brevity of human life was a
favourite theme of fourteenth-century poetry. Almost all medieval lyrics are of
unknown authorship, but the lullaby has traditionally been a women's poetic form.*

An adult lullaby

Lullay, lullay, little child, why weepest thou so sore?
Needs must thou weep—it was ordained thee yore
Ever to live in sorrow, and sigh and mourn alway
As thine elders did before thee in their day.
Lullay, lullay, little child, child, lullay, lullow,
In a strange world a stranger art thou.

Beast and birds, the fish in the flood,
And every living creature, made of bone and blood,
When they come to the world, do themselves some good,
All but the wretched child that is of Adam's brood.
Lullay, lullay, little child, to care thou art born
Thou knowest not this world's waste before thee lies forlorn.

Child, if it betide that thou shalt wealthy be,
Think thou wert fostered on thy mother's knee;
Ever have in mind and heart these things three:
Whence thou comest, what thou art, and what shall come of thee.
Lullay, lullay, little child, lullay, lullay,
With sorrow thou camest into the world, with sorrow shalt wend away.

Trust not to this world: it is thy great foe,
The rich it makes poor, the poor rich also,
It turneth woe to weal, and also weal to woe;
Let no man trust this world while it turneth so.
Lullay, lullay, little child, thy foot is in the wheel:
Thou knowest not where it turns, to woe or to weal.

Child, thou art a pilgrim, in sin thy mother bore thee;
Thou wanderest in this false world—look well before thee!
Death shall come with a blast, out of his dark door,
Adam's kin down to cast, as he hath done before.
Lullay, lullay, little child, so Adam wove thy woe
In the land of Paradise, through Satan our foe.

Child, thou art no pilgrim, but a foreign guest:
Thy days are told, thy journey's die is cast.
Whither thou shalt wend, to north or to east,
Death shall come to thee with sore grief in thy breast.
Lullay, lullay, little child, this sorrow Adam wrought
When he of the apple ate that Eve to him brought.

MARY LAMB

The first tooth

Sister:
Through the house what busy joy,
Just because the infant boy
Has a tiny tooth to show.
I have got a double row,
All as white and all as small;
Yet no one cares for mine at all.
He can say but half a word,
Yet that single sound's preferr'd
To all the words that I can say
In the longest summer day.
He cannot walk, yet if he put
With mimic motion out his foot,
As if he thought he were advancing,
It's prized more than my best dancing.

Brother:
Sister, I know, you jesting are,
Yet O! of jealousy beware.
If the smallest seed should be
In your mind of jealousy,
It will spring, and it will shoot,
Till it bear the baneful fruit.
I remember you, my dear,
Young as is this infant here.
There was not a tooth of those
Your pretty even ivory rows,
But as anxiously was watched,
Till it burst its shell new hatched,
As if it a Phoenix were,
Or some other wonder rare.
So when you began to walk—
So when you began to talk—
As now, the same encomiums past.
'Tis not fitting this should last
Longer than our infant days;
A child is fed with milk and praise.

GEORGE ELIOT
1819–80

'George Eliot' was the pen name of Mary Ann Evans, daughter of a Warwickshire estate manager. Friendships with Coventry intellectuals widened her horizons, but also led to a break with her early faith, though she retained a strong sympathy with her Nonconformist roots. She became assistant editor of a London magazine; there she met writer George Henry Lewes who was separated from his wife. She lived with him for twenty-four years. Only at thirty-nine did she start writing fiction, going on to become one of England's greatest novelists. This poem is made more poignant by the fact that her brother, portrayed as Tom in The Mill on the Floss, refused all contact while she lived with Lewes, seeing her again only after Lewes' death, when she married John Cross, twenty years her junior. She died only months later.

from Brother and sister

1   I cannot choose but think upon the time
      When our two lives grew like two buds that kiss
      At lightest thrill from the bee's swinging chime,
      Because the one so near the other is.

      He was the elder and a little man
      Of forty inches, bound to show no dread,
      And I the girl that puppy-like now ran,
      Now lagged behind my brother's larger tread.

      I held him wise, and when he talked to me
      Of snakes and birds, and which God loved the best,
      I thought his knowledge marked the boundary
      Where men grew blind, though angels knew the rest.

        If he said 'Hush!' I tried to hold my breath;
        Wherever he said 'Come!' I stepped in faith.

2   Long years have left their writing on my brow,
      But yet the freshness and the dew-fed beam
      Of those young mornings are about me now,
      When we two wandered toward the far-off stream

      With rod and line. Our basket held a store
      Baked for us only, and I thought with joy
      That I should have my share, though he had more,
      Because he was the elder and a boy.

The firmaments of daisies since to me
Have had those mornings in their opening eyes,
The bunched cowslip's pale transparency
Carries that sunshine of sweet memories,

> And wild-rose branches take their finest scent
> From those blest hours of infantine content.

*

9   We had the self-same world enlarged for each
By loving difference of girl and boy:
The fruit that hung on high beyond my reach
He plucked for me, and oft he must employ

A measuring glance to guide my tiny shoe
Where lay firm stepping-stones, or call to mind
'This thing I like my sister may not do,
For she is little, and I must be kind.'

Thus boyish Will the nobler mastery learned
Where inward vision over impulse reigns,
Widening its life with separate life discerned,
A Like unlike, a Self that self restrains.

> His years with others must the sweeter be
> For those brief days he spent in loving me.

10 School parted us; we never found again
That childish world where our two spirits mingled
Like scents from varying roses that remain
One sweetness, nor can evermore be singled.

Yet the twin habit of that early time
Lingered for long about the heart and tongue:
We had been natives of one happy clime
And its dear accent to our utterance clung.

Till the dire years whose awful name is Change
Had grasped our souls still yearning in divorce,
And pitiless shaped them in two forms that range
To elements which sever their life's course.

> But were another childhood-world my share,
> I would be born a little sister there.

PATIENCE TUCKWELL
Born 1943

An educational therapist, Patience has worked in schools in Newcastle, Nigeria, Birmingham, Oxfordshire and Israel. She has also travelled in the USA 'because they integrated mentally handicapped children and I so hated our system'. She is herself now disabled by multiple sclerosis, but has recently gained a first class Open University degree 'like Jacob, after seven years'.

New every day

I'd never wish my childhood back to me.
But there at least we knew the laws
that ruled the universe of every day, when we, being tied, were free.
Poverty, dependency, best friends, go side by side;
we were only children and, for children, someone can decide.

I hope that they still
give this great freedom of the will
to kids who only need to concentrate
upon what's on the plate.
You cannot fight the dragons of tomorrow
till tomorrow comes,
because you don't know what they are...
today is sums.

My early schooling is a parable
of something given before we knew the need.
The blackboard cleaned in chalky clouds,
erasing name and deed;
forgotten was forgiven.

And chairs
stacked on top of little desks,
and prayers...
hands together, eyes not quite closed
and then a chanted spell,
our sing-song farewell.
And then...The Bell.

It burst like dams the classrooms
and corridors, rivers, flowed with us.
Cloakrooms and the clang
of buckets said the rule of school
cleaners had begun.

They swept us out towards the gate,
where our mothers, outlaws,
waited.
Then, long after, very late,
Night, like a caretaker
locked all the doors.

Piecemeal we lived, new every day
and kept no scores.
All our fights were silly little ones.
Battles, not wars.

EVANGELINE PATERSON
Born 1928

Evangeline was born in Limavady and grew up in Dublin, but she married an Englishman and has lived in Scotland, Leicester, South Africa and now north-east England. She has been deeply involved in the revival of the arts among evangelical Christians. Evangeline has won major poetry prizes, including a Cheltenham Festival prize. Her collections Bringing the Water Hyacinth to Africa *and* Lucifer at the Fair *are published by Taxus Press.*

Variations on a street song

Ten little girls from school are we,
plaited, pony-tailed, socks to the knee.
Some are as smart as smart can be,
and each one of us is pretty.

Rosie Fagan says she'll cry
if she doesn't get the fellow with the roving eye.
Elsie Geraghty says she'll die
for want of the Golden City.

*The wind, the wind, the wind blows high
the rain comes tumbling from the sky.*

Some are bound to travel far,
go through the world like a shooting star.
Some will shunt like an old street car.

Some will fall right over the edge
to the place where all the nightmares lodge.
Some will always cling to a ledge.

*The wind, the wind, the wind blows high
the snow comes drifting from the sky.*

Some get pudding and still want pie.
Some settle for a fellow with a roving eye,
and some will pine and some will die
for want of the Golden City.

MARGARET CAVENDISH, DUCHESS OF NEWCASTLE
?1623–73

'I would rather die in the adventure of noble achievements than live in obscure and sluggish security,' wrote Margaret. Shy in private—she called herself 'Mistress Bashful'—in public she was exhibitionist, designing her own exotic clothing and nicknamed 'Mad Madge'. Margaret Lucas' early life was troubled by political events. Her home was destroyed in a riot and her family imprisoned. During the Civil War she fled to Brittany as lady-in-waiting to Queen Henrietta Maria. In exile she met William Cavendish, thirty years older and 'the only person I was ever in love with'. They lived in poverty in Paris and Holland, returning to England at the Restoration. She published eleven books, including philosophy, poetry, drama and a biography of her husband.

A posset for Nature's breakfast

Life scums the cream of beauty with Time's spoon,
And draws the claret-wine of blushes soon;
Then boils it in a skillet clean of youth,
And thicks it well with crumbled bread of truth;
Sets it upon the fire of life which does
Burn clearer much when Health her bellows blows;
Then takes the eggs of fair and bashful eyes,
And puts them in a countenance that's wise,
Cuts in a lemon of the sharpest wit—
Discretion as a knife is used for it.
A handful of chaste thoughts, double refined,
Six spoonsful of a noble and gentle mind,
A grain of mirth to give't a little taste,
Then takes it off for fear the substance waste,
And puts it in a basin of good health,
And with this meat doth Nature please herself.

REBEKAH CARMICHAEL
Writing 1790–1806

Robert Burns was among the supporters who paid for the book to appear when Rebekah's poems were published in Scotland by the 'subscription' method. Her poems suggest that she was orphaned at an early age. She married a Mr Hay but was soon widowed and left destitute with a son. Her last known writing is a letter to her publisher, enclosing a poem and asking for a loan 'in my illness'.

The tooth

O look not, lady, with disdain!
    Nor fill our hearts with ruth;
You still may charm some humble swain,
    Although you've lost a tooth!

Thy beaming eyes are black as jet,
    And pretty is thy mouth;
No angel ever smiled so sweet,
    Before you lost a tooth.

While fondly thus you strive to shine
    In all the charms of youth,
Your face and figure are divine,
    But oh! you've lost a tooth.

Ah! why that angry frown? for shame!
    I only speak the truth:
It cannot hurt Eliza's fame
    To say she's lost a tooth.

But search some hearts, perhaps you'll find
    A greater fault, forsooth;
Oh! it were well for womankind
    Were all their loss a tooth!

DOLLIE RADFORD

1858–?

Dollie Maitland was married to fellow-poet Ernest Radford and published several collections of poetry from her early thirties on.

Soliloquy of a maiden aunt

The ladies bow, and partners set,
And turn around and pirouette
    And trip the Lancers.

But no one seeks my ample chair,
Or asks me with persuasive air
    To join the dancers.

They greet me, as I sit alone
Upon my solitary throne,
    And pass politely.

Yet mine could keep the measured beat,
As surely as the youngest feet,
    And tread as lightly.

No other maiden had my skill
In our old homestead on the hill—
    That merry May-time

When Allan closed the flagging ball,
And danced with me before them all,
    Until the day-time.

Again I laugh, and step alone,
And curtsey low as on my own
    His strong hand closes.

But Allan now seeks staid delight,
His son there, brought my niece tonight
    These early roses.

Time orders well, we have our Spring,
Our songs, and may-flower gathering,
    Our love and laughter.

And children chatter all the while,
And leap the brook and climb the stile
    And follow after.

And yet—the step of Allan's son
Is not as light as was the one
    That went before it.

And that old lace, I think, falls down
Less softly on Priscilla's gown
    Than when I wore it.

ELMA MITCHELL
Born 1919

A native of Airdrie, Scotland, Elma Mitchell now lives in Somerset. She is a professional librarian who has also worked in broadcasting, publishing and journalism. She has published four collections of which People Etcetera *contains selections from earlier volumes as well as many new poems.*

The corset

The corset came today. I cannot wear it.

What are your difficulties, may I ask?
A slight constriction round about the heart?
That, at your time of life, you must expect,
The back and shoulders mainly take the weight,
Astonishingly comfortable, on the whole
And really very stylish,—for your size.
This line is very flattering to the bust,
And this delineates what was once a waist,
And further down, you see, complete control...

You'll soon acquire the knack; just slip it on,
Wriggle, distort, contract - that's right, that's it.
Now you are one smooth mould from head to thighs.
You'll be surprised how good it makes you feel...

The corset came today. I will not wear it.
Come, lumpish lumbering muscles, to your task,
Unsupple wits, turn sinuous again,
Or live as limp and cripple, but let live.

7 The Last Enemy

ANNE BRADSTREET
?1612–1672

The Tenth Muse Lately Sprung Up in America *was the bold title of Anne's poems
published anonymously in England by her brother-in-law. Probably born in
Northampton, the daughter of the Earl of Lincoln's steward, she and all her family
emigrated to New England two years after her marriage at sixteen to Simon
Bradstreet. Both her father and her husband became governors of Massachusetts Bay.
However the Bradstreets lived in some hardship, bringing up eight children in primitive
conditions. Her poems reflect the struggles of childbirth, death of infants, the burning
of her house, and yet they also express a firm faith.*

In memory of my dear grandchild Elizabeth Bradstreet, who deceased August, 1665, being a year and a half old

Farewell, dear babe, my heart's too much content,
Farewell sweet babe, the pleasure of mine eye,
Farewell fair flower that for a space was lent,
Then ta'en away into Eternity.
Blest babe, why should I once bewail thy fate,
Or sigh thy days so soon were terminate,
Since thou art settled in an everlasting state?

By nature trees do rot when they are grown,
And plums and apples thoroughly ripe do fall,
And corn and grass are in their season mown,
And time brings down what is both strong and tall.
But plants new set to be eradicate,
And buds new blown to have so short a date,
Is by His hand alone that guides nature and fate.

EMILY BRONTË
1818–49

It is Emily's Wuthering Heights *which, of all the three Brontë sisters' work, most powerfully captures the stern beauty and fascination of the Yorkshire moors. The book also reveals its author's passionate and imaginative nature, impatient of restraint and finding meaning in nature mysticism rather than orthodox Christian faith. Like Charlotte, Emily finished her patchy schooling in Brussels and was briefly and unhappily a governess. Her novel appeared not long before she died of tuberculosis, having refused to see a doctor or even go to bed.*

My lady's grave

The linnet in the rocky dells,
The moor-lark in the air,
The bee among the heather bells
That hide my lady fair:

The wild deer browse above her breast;
The wild birds raise their brood;
And they, her smiles of love caress'd,
Have left her solitude!

I ween that when the grave's dark wall
Did first her form retain,
They thought their hearts could ne'er recall
The light of joy again.

They thought the tide of grief would flow
Uncheck'd through future years;
But where is all their anguish now,
And where are all their tears?

Well, let them fight for honour's breath,
Or pleasure's shade pursue—
The dweller in the land of death
Is changed and careless too.

And if their eyes should watch and weep
Till sorrow's source were dry,
She would not, in her tranquil sleep,
Return a single sigh!

Blow, west wind, by the lonely mound:
And murmur, summer streams!
There is no need of other sound
To soothe my lady's dreams.

EMILY DICKINSON
1830–86

Eternity, I'm coming

A wife at daybreak I shall be,
Sunrise, thou hast a flag for me?
At midnight I am yet a maid—
How short it takes to make it bride!
Then, Midnight, I have passed from thee
Unto the East and Victory.

Midnight, 'Good night'
I hear thee call.
The angels bustle in the hall,
Softly my Future climbs the stair,
I fumble at my childhood's prayer—
So soon to be a child no more!
Eternity, I'm coming, sir—
Master, I've seen that face before.

SARAH WILLIAMS
1841–1868

Deep-sea soundings

Mariner, what of the deep?
    This of the deep:
Twilight is there, and solemn, changeless calm;
Beauty is there, and tender healing balm—
Balm with no root in earth, or air, or sea,
Poised by the finger of God, it floateth free,
And, as it threads the waves, the sound doth rise,—
Hither shall come no further sacrifice;
Never again the anguished clutch at life,
Never again great Love and Death in strife;
He who hath suffered all, need fear no more,
Quiet his portion now, for evermore.

Mariner, what of the deep?
    This of the deep:
Solitude dwells not there, though silence reign;
Mighty the brotherhood of loss and pain;
There is communion past the need of speech,
There is a love no words of love can reach;
Heavy the waves that superincumbent press,
But as we labour here with constant stress,
Hand doth hold out to hand not help alone,
But the deep bliss of being fully known.
There are no kindred like the kin of sorrow,
There is no hope like theirs who fear no morrow.

Mariner, what of the deep?
    This of the deep:
Though we have travelled past the line of day,
Glory of night doth light us on our way,
Radiance that comes we know not how nor whence,
Rainbows without the rain, past duller sense,
Music of hidden reefs and waves long past,
Thunderous organ tones from far-off blast,
Harmony, victrix, throned in state sublime,
Couched on the wrecks be-gemmed with pearls of time;
Never a wreck but brings some beauty here;
Down where the waves are stilled the sea shines clear;
Deeper than life the plan of life doth lie,
He who knows all, fears naught. Great Death shall die.

MARY COLERIDGE
1861–1907

A great-niece of Samuel Taylor Coleridge, Mary was born in London to a well-off family and was educated at home, partly by the poet William Cory (who wrote the 'Eton Boating Song', not an obvious influence on Mary's work!). Reading Tolstoy gave her a concern for the poor and she taught working women at home and later at the Working Women's College. She wrote five historical novels, a volume of essays and many poems which show a strongly-held faith, intense feeling and powerful imagination.

There

There, in that other world, what waits for me?
What shall I find after that other birth?
No stormy, tossing, foaming, smiling sea,
    But a new earth.

No sun to mark the changing of the days,
No slow, soft falling of the alternate night,
No moon, no star, no light upon my ways,
    Only the Light.

No gray cathedral, wide and wondrous fair,
That I may tread where all my fathers trod.
Nay, nay, my soul, no house of God is there,
    But only God.

CHARLOTTE MEW
1861–1928

'Charlotte Mew, said to be a writer' was the brief obituary notice on the death of this self-effacing poet and short story writer. Although greatly admired by Thomas Hardy who, with John Masefield and Walter de la Mare, secured her a Civil List pension in 1922, she had little confidence in her own abilities. Always troubled by illness and family worries, she committed suicide after her sister's death in 1928.

Old shepherd's prayer

Up to the bed by the window, where I be lyin',
Comes bells and bleat of the flock wi' they two children's clack.
Over, from under the eaves there's the starlings flyin',
And down in yard, fit to burst his chain, yapping out at Sue I do hear young
    Mac.

Turning around like a falled-over sack
I can see team ploughin' up in Whithy-bush field and meal carts startin' up
    road to Church-Town;
Saturday arternoon the men goin' back
And the women from market, trapin' home over the down.

Heavenly Master, I wud like to wake to they same green places
Where I know'd for breakin' dogs and follerin' sheep,
And if I may not walk in th'old ways and look on th'old faces
I wud sooner sleep.

FRANCES CORNFORD
1886–1960

Frances Crofts came from illustrious forebears: Charles Darwin was her paternal grandfather and her mother was a lecturer at the newly-founded Newnham College for women in Cambridge. Frances married Francis Cornford, Professor of Ancient Philosophy, and lived in Cambridge most of her life. Her son John was killed on his twenty-first birthday in 1936, during the Spanish Civil War. Nine collections of her work were published and she was awarded the Queen's Medal for Poetry in 1959.

All Souls' night

My love came back to me
Under the November tree
Shelterless and dim.
He put his hand upon my shoulder,
He did not think me strange or older,
Nor I, him.

VERONICA ZUNDEL
Born 1953

This 'circular' poem was written when her colleague Tim Dean was admitted to hospital with leukaemia in February 1985.

Lent

lean years
till you took me
indoors
like a waif
fed me fair work and
fine-tuned words

my soul grew full and easy under your sunlight
rare shadows sharpening sweetness

now you lie
in a narrow bed
in the shriven season
sterile tubes supply
your small sustenance

the days are long to Easter

between us falls
the mind's darkness
my love cannot cross
these long white halls
calls
lost in the echoes

your wife brings me news like
crumbs to the starving

alone bearing each day
your burden
watching the calendar
turn
I learn
a hard teaching:

you were never
to me
given
but

PART TWO

Her Neighbours

'Being a woman,' said Joseph Conrad, 'is a terribly difficult trade, since it consists principally of dealing with men.' For generations, this was literally true. Marriage was the only 'career' for middle- and upper-class women; working-class women had a little more independence, but male protection of some kind was the only sure means of survival.

The sexes were created as partners, but too often have acted as masters and servants. So it is not surprising that the poets in this section often look wryly on the 'other half' of the human race. Yet there is sympathy, too—for the man who must conform to the stereotype of the 'hero', who may be just as lonely in marriage as his wife, who must battle to scrape a living. There is appreciation of the work men do and the support they provide. And some poems testify that women and men can find fulfilment in a loving, committed partnership.

Of course, being human is itself a difficult trade, consisting mainly of dealing with other humans... These poems also reflect on the delights and sorrows of mothers and children; the ups and downs of relations with friends, sisters, brothers; the battle for justice for neighbours both male and female, black and white. In the process they comment, explicitly and implicitly, on women's place in society, and look to a future when their rightful place will be that of equals.

8 The Other Half

MARION PITMAN
Born 1955

'Is any man strong enough not to be afraid of a woman who tells the truth?' asks Marion in one poem. 'Telling the truth' is a major concern of her work, which often confronts the polite evasions by which we keep each other at a distance. Brought up in London, she currently keeps a secondhand bookshop in Twickenham. She has won various poetry prizes, including first prize in the 1985 Christian Poetry Competition, and has published a collection of her poems called Lunch with Veronica.

Hero

and when he died his mother's grief was a public show
replete with public sympathy
His father, locked in his private room
cried out his broken heart alone
till he had no tears left
then went out dry eyed
How brave his father is they said How brave.

ELIZABETH BARRETT BROWNING
1806-61

A man's requirements

Love me, Sweet, with all thou art,
Feeling, thinking, seeing;
Love me in the lightest part,
Love me in full being.

Love me with thine open youth
In its frank surrender;
With the vowing of thy mouth,
With its silence tender.

Love me with thine azure eyes,
Made for earnest granting;
Taking colour from the skies,
Can Heaven's truth be wanting?

Love me with their lids, that fall
Snow-like at first meeting;
Love me with thine heart, that all
Neighbours then see beating.

Love me with thine hand stretched out
Freely - open minded:
Love me with thy loitering foot,—
Hearing one behind it.

Love me with thy voice, that turns
Sudden faint above me;
Love me with thy blush that burns
When I murmur, Love me!

Love me with thy thinking soul,
Break it to love-sighing;
Love me with thy thoughts that roll
On through living—dying.

Love me in thy gorgeous airs,
When the world has crowned thee;
Love me, kneeling at thy prayers,
With the angels round thee.

Love me pure, as musers do,
Up the woodlands shady:
Love me gaily, fast and true,
As a winsome lady.

Through all hopes that keep us brave,
Further off or nigher,
Love me for the house and grave,—
And for something higher.

Thus, if thou wilt prove me, Dear,
Woman's love no fable,
I will love thee—half a year—
As a man is able.

EDITH NESBIT
1858–1924

Villeggiature

My window, framed in pear-tree bloom,
White-curtained shone, and softly lighted:
So, by the pear-tree, to my room
Your ghost last night climbed uninvited.

Your solid self, long leagues away,
Deep in dull books, had hardly missed me;
And yet you found this Romeo's way,
And through the blossom climbed and kissed me.

I watched the still and dewy lawn,
The pear-tree boughs hung white above you;
I listened to you till the dawn,
And half forgot I did not love you.

Oh, dear! what pretty things you said,
What pearls of song you threaded for me!
I did not—till your ghost had fled—
Remember how you always bore me!

LADY MARGARET SACKVILLE
1881–1963

Third daughter of the seventh Earl de la Warr, Lady Margaret lived most of her life in Edinburgh, moving to Cheltenham in her later years. She wrote numerous volumes of poetry, mainly for children.

The apple

Eve, smiling, pluck'd the apple, then
Laugh'd, sigh'd—and tasted it again:
'Strange such a pleasant, juicy thing
On a forbidden tree should spring!'

But had she seen with clearer eyes,
Or had the serpent been less wise,
She'd scarce have shown such little wit
As to let Adam taste of it!

RUTH PITTER
Born 1897

Daughter of two teachers, educated in east London, Ruth worked in the War Office and then in an arts and crafts firm on the east coast, before setting up her own craft business in Chelsea. She was encouraged in her writing by Hilaire Belloc; two of her collections of poetry won major awards, and she was given the Queen's Gold Medal for Poetry in 1955. Nature and her Christian faith are central to her work, but humour is also vital, especially in her 'cat poems'.

The Irish patriarch

He bathes his soul in women's wrath;
His whiskers twinkle, and it seems
As if he trod some airy path
In that young land of warriors' dreams;
As if he took a needle-bath
In mountain falls, in tingling streams.

The man whom nagging drives to drink
Should learn from him, whom female rage
Seems but to make a precious link
With some sweet ancient heritage,
With women saying—huh!—what they think!
To the amusement of the sage.

O women, what a boon it is,
With workday worries at their worst,
When hordes of little miseries
Force us to speak our mind or burst,
To be Rich-angered Mistresses,
Not Shrews and Vixens, Cross and Curst!

PHYLLIS McGINLEY
1905–1978

'No man could have written them,' said W.H.Auden of Phyllis McGinley's poems.
Beneath her deceptively 'light' verse forms lurk profound insights into the ironies and
pleasures of everyday life, the vicissitudes of women's lives, and the foibles of men.
Born in Oregon, a Roman Catholic, she graduated from the University of Utah,
worked as an English teacher, an advertising copywriter and a poetry editor, and
wrote for children and adults. Her collection of poems from three decades, Times
Three, *won the Pulitzer Prize in 1960.*

First lesson
from A girl's-eye view of relatives

The thing to remember about fathers is, they're men.
A girl has to keep it in mind.
They are dragon-seekers, bent on improbable rescues.
Scratch any father, you'll find
Someone chock-full of qualms and romantic terrors,
Believing change is a threat—
Like your first shoes with heels on, like your first bicycle
It took such months to get.

Walk in strange woods, they warn you about the snakes there.
Climb, and they fear you'll fall.
Books, angular boys, or swimming in deep water—
Fathers mistrust them all.
Men are the worriers. It is difficult for them
To learn what they must learn:
How you have a journey to take and very likely,
For a while, will not return.

9 Love's Joy

ELIZABETH TOLLETT
1694–1754

Elizabeth spent her early years in the Tower of London, where her father, commissioner of the Navy, had a house. Noticing her talents, he gave her a good education in music, drawing, languages, history, poetry and mathematics. She published poems in English and Latin, and a verse drama, Susanna; or Innocence Preserved. *Her learning, said a contemporary, 'was dignified by an unfeigned piety and the moral virtues which she possessed and practised in an eminent degree'.*

Winter song

Ask me no more, my truth to prove,
What I would suffer for my love.
With thee I would in exile go
To regions of eternal snow,
O'er floods by solid ice confined,
Through forest bare with northern wind:
While all around my eyes I cast,
Where all is wild and all is waste.
If there the tim'rous stag you chase,
Or rouse to fight a fiercer race,
Undaunted I thy arms would bear,
And give thy hand the hunter's spear.
When the low sun withdraws his light,
And menaces an half-year's night,
The conscious moon and stars above
Shall guide me with my wandering love.
Beneath the mountain's hollow brow,
Or in its rocky cells below,
Thy rural feast I would provide,
Nor envy palaces their pride.
The softest moss should dress thy bed,
With savage spoils about thee spread:
While faithful love the watch should keep,
To banish danger from thy sleep.

SUSANNA BLAMIRE
1747–94

'The Muse of Cumberland' was the title popularly given to this farmer's daughter—perhaps inappropriately, since she was a poet in her own right, not merely an inspiration to others. In spite of acclaim in her lifetime, her poems were not collected until 1842. The poems give a vivid picture of contemporary Cumbrian life; some, like this one, are songs in the Scottish dialect.

The siller crown

'And ye sall walk in silk attire,
And siller hae to spare,
Gin ye'll consent to be his bride,
Nor think o' Donald mair.'

O, wha wad buy a silken gown
Wi' a puir broken heart?
Or what's to me a siller crown
Gin frae my love I part?

The mind whose meanest wish is pure
Far dearest is to me,
And ere I'm forced to break my faith,
I'll lay me down and dee.

For I hae vowed a virgin's vow
My lover's faith to share,
An' he has gi'en to me his heart,
An' what can man do mair?

His mind and manners won my heart,
He gratefu' took the gift,
An' did I wish to seek it back
It wad be waur than theft.

The langest life can ne'er repay
The love he bears to me,
And ere I'm forced to break my faith,
I'll lay me down and dee.

ELIZABETH BARRETT BROWNING

1806–61

Elizabeth's 'Sonnets from the Portuguese' are, of course, entirely her own. Inventing a Portuguese original was a way, perhaps a typically female way, of disclaiming authorship of these passionate love poems.

Sonnets from the Portuguese, no. 3

Go from me. Yet I feel that I shall stand
Henceforward in thy shadow. Nevermore
Alone upon the threshold of my door
Of individual life I shall command
The uses of my soul, nor lift my hand
Serenely in the sunshine as before,
Without the sense of that which I forbore—
Thy touch upon the palm. The widest land
Doom takes to part us, leaves thy heart in mine
With pulses that beat double. What I do
And what I dream include thee, as the wine
Must taste of its own grapes. And when I sue
God for myself, He hears that name of thine,
And sees within my eyes the tears of two.

CAROLINE NORTON
1808–77

Granddaughter of the playwright Sheridan, and sister of fellow poet Helena, Lady Dufferin, Caroline was unhappily married to the Hon. G. C. Norton, and the couple separated. Her experience led her to campaign for a change in the laws on married women's property rights and the custody of children, and two of her novels aimed to further this cause. She was eventually successful in bringing about some changes. In 1877 she married the art historian Sir William Stirling-Maxwell.

I do not love thee

I do not love thee!—no! I do not love thee!
And yet when thou art absent I am sad;
And envy even the bright blue sky above thee,
Whose quiet stars may see thee and be glad.

I do not love thee!—yet, I know not why,
Whate'er thou dost seems still well done, to me:
And often in my solitude I sigh
That those I do love are not more like thee!

I do not love thee!—yet, when thou art gone,
I hate the sound (though those who speak be dear)
Which breaks the lingering echo of the tone
Thy voice of music leaves upon my ear.

I do not love thee!—yet thy speaking eyes,
With their deep, bright, and most expressive blue,
Between me and the midnight heaven arise,
Oftener than any eyes I ever knew.

I know I do not love thee! yet, alas!
Others will scarcely trust my candid heart;
And oft I catch them smiling as they pass,
Because they see me gazing where thou art.

JEAN INGELOW

1820–97

A banker's daughter born in Boston, Lincolnshire, Jean spent her later life in London.
She published several novels and three books of poems, many in the style of ballads.
They made her immensely popular at the time, though she is almost forgotten today.

The long white seam

As I came round the harbour buoy,
The lights began to gleam,
No wave the land-locked water stirred,
The crags were white as cream:
And I marked my love by candle-light
Sewing her long white seam.
    It's aye sewing ashore, my dear,
    Watch and steer at sea,
    It's reef and furl, and haul the line,
    Set sail, and think of thee.

I climbed to reach her cottage door;
O sweetly my love sings!
Like a shaft of light her voice breaks forth,
My soul to meet it springs
As the shining water leaped of old,
When stirred by angel wings.
    Aye longing to list anew,
    Awake and in my dream,
    But never a song she sang like this,
    Sewing her long white seam.

Fair fall the lights, the harbour lights,
That brought me in to thee,
And peace drop down on that low roof
For the sight that I did see,
And the voice, my dear, that rang so clear
All for the love of me.
    For O, for O, with brows bent low
    By the candle's flickering gleam,
    Her wedding gown it was she wrought,
    Sewing the long white seam.

CHRISTINA ROSSETTI
1830–94

A birthday

My heart is like a singing bird
Whose nest is in a water'd shoot;
My heart is like an apple-tree
Whose boughs are bent with thick-set fruit;
My heart is like a rainbow shell
That paddles in a halcyon sea;
My heart is gladder than all these,
Because my love is come to me.

Raise me a dais of silk and down;
Hang it with vair[1] and purple dyes;
Carve it in doves and pomegranates,
And peacocks with a hundred eyes;
Work it in gold and silver grapes,
In leaves and silver fleurs-de-lys;
Because the birthday of my life
Is come, my love is come to me.

[1] Vair = a squirrel fur much used in medieval times

MARY COLERIDGE
1861–1907

A moment

The clouds had made a crimson crown
About the mountains high.
The stormy sun was going down
In a stormy sky.

Why did you let your eyes so rest on me,
And hold your breath between?
In all the ages this can never be
As if it had not been.

ANNE RIDLER
Born 1912

Born in Warwickshire, the daughter of a teacher at Rugby School, Anne Bradby was educated at Downe House School and King's College, London. She married Vivian Ridler in 1938 and they have two sons and two daughters. She was secretary to T.S.Eliot (who influenced her poetry) and a member of the editorial department of the publishers Faber & Faber. Anne has published many collections of poetry, five plays and a scholarly edition of the works of Thomas Traherne.

Villanelle for the middle of the way

When we first love, his eyes reflect our own;
When mirrors change to windows we can see;
Seeing, we know how much is still unknown.

Was it a trite reflection? What is shown
When we gaze deep begins the mystery:
When we first love, his eyes reflect our own.

Neither of us could cast the first stone,
And to forgive is tender. 'Now', thought we,
'Seeing, we know.' How much was still unknown

We later learnt. But by forgiveness grown—
As Blake discovered—apt for eternity,
Though in first love his eyes reflect our own.

What was the crime for which you would atone
Or could be crime now between you and me
Seeing we know how much is still unknown?

I know you now by heart not eyes alone,
Dearer the dry than even the green tree.
When we first love, his eyes reflect our own,
Seeing, we know how much is still unknown.

10 Love's Sorrow

QUEEN ELIZABETH I
1533–1603

England's 'virgin queen', daughter of Henry VIII and Anne Boleyn, was well read in Latin, Greek, French and Italian, and translated works of ancient literature. Like any educated person of her day, she wrote poetry as a matter of course, even scratching a verse on a window with a diamond when she was imprisoned as a young princess. She refused all offers of marriage, partly for political reasons (perhaps also because, as is thought, she loved Robert Dudley, Earl of Leicester who was already married). She saw herself as married to her kingdom, which she restored to stability and prosperity. Elizabeth ruled during one of the most flourishing periods of English history. She was fiercely committed to her Protestant faith.

Importune me no more

When I was fair and young and favour graced me,
Of many was I sought their mistress for to be,
But I did scorn them all and answered them therefore,
Go, go, go, seek some other where,
    Importune me no more.

How many weeping eyes I made to pine with woe,
How many sighing hearts I have no skill to show,
Yet I the prouder grew, and answered them therefore,
Go, go, go, seek some other where,
    Importune me no more.

Then spake fair Venus' son, that proud victorious boy,
And said, fine dame since that you have been so coy,
I will go pluck your plumes that you shall say no more,
Go, go, go, seek some other where,
    Importune me no more.

When he had spake these words such change grew in my breast,
That neither day nor night since that I could take any rest,
Then lo, I did repent of that I said before,
Go, go, go, seek some other where,
    Importune me no more.

APHRA BEHN
1640–89

The first English woman to make her living by writing, Aphra Johnson was the daughter of a Kent barber who emigrated to Surinam. Returning to London at eighteen, Aphra married Mr Behn, a Dutch merchant, but was widowed at twenty-six. She was then employed by the court as a spy in Antwerp. Back in London again, she made literary friends, and wrote many bawdy but highly popular plays, as well as novels which include Oronooko, *about the famous slave whom she had met in Surinam.*

And forgive us our trespasses

How prone we are to sin, how sweet were made
The pleasures, our resistless hearts invade!
Of all my crimes, the breach of all thy laws,
Love, soft bewitching love! has been the cause;
Of all the paths that vanity has trod,
That sure will soonest be forgiven of God;
If things on earth may be to heaven resembled,
It must be love, pure, constant, undissembled:
But if to sin perchance the charmer press,
Forgive, O Lord, forgive our trespasses.

An earl's daughter, Anne wrote this famous poem to an old tune in a fit of loneliness after her sister's marriage. It was her sister Elizabeth who suggested 'Steal the cow' (third stanza), when Anne demanded 'a fifth sorrow in the four lines' for her unfortunate heroine. In her early forties Anne married Andrew Barnard, a younger man, who became Colonial Secretary in Cape Town. Her letters from South Africa were published seventy-six years after her death. Auld Robin Gray appeared anonymously, but one astute critic deduced it could not be an ancient Scottish ballad as a Scots 'pound' was only twenty pence, less than a crown! Anne eventually admitted her authorship to Walter Scott.

Auld Robin Gray

When the sheep are in the fauld, when the cows come hame,
When a' the weary world to quiet rest are gane,
The woes o' my heart fa' in showers frae my e'e,
Unkenned by my gudeman, who soundly sleeps by me.

Young Jamie lo'ed me weel, and sought me for his bride;
But saving ae crown-piece, he'd naething else beside.
To make the crown a pound, my Jamie gaed to sea;
And the crown and the pound, oh! they were baith for me!

Before he had been gane a twelvemonth and a day,
My father brak his arm, our cow was stown away;
My mither she fell sick—my Jamie was at sea—
And auld Robin Gray, oh! he came a-courtin' me.

My father cou'dna work, my mother cou'dna spin;
I toiled day and night, but their bread I cou'dna win;
And Rob maintain'd them baith, and wi' tears in his e'e
Said, 'Jenny, oh! for their sakes, will you marry me?'

My heart it said na, and I look'd for Jamie back;
But hard blew the winds, and his ship was a wrack;
His ship it was a wrack! Why didna Jenny dee!
Or, wherefore am I spared to cry out, Woe is me!

My father argued sair—my mother didna speak;
But she looked in my face till my heart was like to break:
They gied him my hand, but my heart was in the sea;
And so auld Robin Gray, he was gudeman to me.

I hadna been his wife a week but only four,
When mournfu' as I sat on the stane at my door,
I saw my Jamie's ghaist—for I couldna think it he,
Till he said, 'I'm come hame, my love, to marry thee!'

O sair, sair did we greet, and mickle say of a';
Ae kiss we took, nae mair—I bad him gang awa.
I wish that I were dead, but I'm no like to dee;
For O, I am but young to cry out, Woe is me!

I gang like a ghaist, and I carena much to spin;
I darena think o' Jamie, for that wad be a sin;
But I will do my best a gude wife aye to be,
For auld Robin Gray, oh! he is sae kind to me.

LADY AUGUSTA GREGORY
1852–1932

'In translating these poems I have chosen to do so in the speech of the thatched houses where I have heard and gathered them,' wrote Augusta in the introduction to her 1919 Kiltartan Poetry Book. A rich landowner's daughter and the wife of a member of Parliament and former governor of Ceylon, she became interested in Irish literature both traditional and modern through her meeting with W.B.Yeats. She wrote many short plays for his Abbey Theatre in Dublin.

from Grief of a girl's heart

O Donal Oge, if you go across the sea,
Bring myself with you and do not forget it;
And you will have a sweetheart for fair days and market days,
And the daughter of the King of Greece beside you at night.

It is late last night the dog was speaking of you;
The snipe was speaking of you in her deep marsh.
It is you are the lonely bird through the woods;
And that you may be without a mate until you find me.

You promised me, and you said a lie to me,
That you would be before me where the sheep are flocked;
I gave a whistle and three hundred cries to you,
And I found nothing there but a bleating lamb.

You promised me a thing that was hard for you,
A ship of gold under a silver mast;
Twelve towns with a market in all of them,
And a fine white court by the side of the sea.

You promised me a thing that is not possible,
That you would give me gloves of the skin of a fish;
That you would give me shoes of the skin of a bird;
And a suit of the dearest silk in Ireland.

O Donal Oge, it is I would be better to you
Than a high, proud, spendthrift lady:
I would milk the cow; I would bring help to you;
And if you were hard pressed, I would strike a blow for you.

You have taken the east from me; you have taken the west from me,
You have taken what is before me and what is behind me;
You have taken the moon, you have taken the sun from me,
And my fear is great that you have taken God from me!

CHARLOTTE BRONTË
1816–1855

He saw my heart's woe

He saw my heart's woe, discovered my soul's anguish,
How in fever, in thirst, in atrophy it pined;
Knew he could heal, yet looked and let it languish,
To its moans spirit-deaf, to its pangs spirit-blind.

But once a year he heard a whisper low and dreary,
Appealing for aid, entreating some reply;
Only when sick, soul-worn and torture-weary,
Breathed I that prayer—heard I that sigh.

He was mute as is the grave, he stood stirless as a tower;
At last I looked up, and saw I prayed to stone:
I asked help of that which to help had no power,
I sought love where love was utterly unknown.

Idolater, I kneeled to an idol cut in rock,
I might have slashed my flesh and drawn my heart's best blood,
The Granite God had felt no tenderness, no shock;
My Baal had not seen nor heard nor understood.

In dark remorse I rose. I rose in darker shame,
Self-condemned I withdrew to an exile from my kind;
A solitude I sought where mortal never came,
Hoping in its wilds forgetfulness to find.

Now, Heaven, heal the wound which I still deeply feel;
Thy glorious hosts look not in scorn on our poor race;
Thy King eternal doth no iron judgment deal
On suffering worms who seek forgiveness, comfort, grace.

He gave our hearts to love, he will not love despise,
E'en if the gift be lost, as mine was long ago.
He will forgive the fault, will bid the offender rise,
Wash out with dews of bliss the fiery brand of woe;

And give a sheltered place beneath the unsullied throne,
Whence the soul redeemed may mark Time's fleeting course around earth;
And know its trial overpast, its suffering gone,
And feel the peril past of Death's immortal birth.

Twice

I took my heart in my hand
(O my love, O my love),
I said: Let me fall or stand,
Let me live or die,
But this once hear me speak
(O my love, O my love)—
Yet a woman's words are weak;
You should speak, not I.

You took my heart in your hand
With a friendly smile,
With a critical eye you scann'd,
Then set it down,
And said, 'It is still unripe,
Better wait awhile;
Wait while the skylarks pipe,
Till the corn grows brown.'

As you set it down it broke—
Broke, but I did not wince;
I smiled at the speech you spoke,
At your judgement I heard:
But I have not often smiled
Since then, nor question'd since,
Nor cared for cornflowers wild,
Nor sung with the singing bird.

I take my heart in my hand,
O my God, O my God,
My broken heart in my hand:
Thou hast seen, judge Thou.
My hope was written on sand,
O my God, O my God:
Now let thy judgement stand—
Yea, judge me now.

This contemn'd of a man,
This marr'd one heedless day,
This heart take thou to scan
Both within and without:
Refine with fire its gold,
Purge thou its dross away—
Yea, hold it in Thy hold,
Whence none can pluck it out.

I take my heart in my hand—
I shall not die, but live—
Before Thy face I stand;
I, for Thou callest such:
All that I have I bring,
All that I am I give,
Smile Thou and I shall sing,
But shall not question much.

MARION PITMAN
Born 1955

Polly

Polly, Polly, peacock's eyes
In your hair; your lover sighs

He has brought you nectarines,
Apricocks and muscadines,

He has brought you silks and lace,
Collars jewelled to frame your face,

He has brought you linen fine,
Golden rings and Spanish wine;

Minstrels has he sent to play
By your window, night and day;

Jewels has he brought a score,
Yet—you long for something more?

Tell me, Polly, is he cold?
Hard and loveless as his gold?

Or it may be, he is old,
Youth and passion spent and sold?

Polly, is he cruel? or coarse?
Cowardly? a fool?—or worse?

No. Only that in his eyes
No shadow of heaven lies.

11 Marriage

ANNE BRADSTREET
1612–72

To my dear and loving husband

If ever two were one, then surely we.
If ever man were lov'd by wife, then thee;
If ever wife was happy in a man,
Compare me with ye women if you can.
I prize thy love more than whole mines of gold,
Or all the riches that the East doth hold.
My love is such that rivers cannot quench,
Nor aught but love from thee, give recompense.
Thy love is such I can no way repay,
The heavens reward thee manifold, I pray.
Then while we live, in love let's so persever
That, when we live no more, we may live ever.

APHRA BEHN
?1640–89

Song

As wretched, vain and indiscreet
Those matches I deplore,
Whose bartering friends in counsel meet
To huddle in a wedding sheet
Some miserable pair that never met before.

Poor love of no account must be,
Though ne'er so fix'd and true.
No merit but in gold they see;
So portion and estate agree,
No matter what the bride and bridegroom do.

Curs'd may all covetous husbands be
That wed with such design,
And curs'd they are; for while they ply
Their wealth, some lover by the by
Reaps the true bliss, and digs the richer mine.

*'To form the minds of my children' was Mary Barber's stated aim in writing poetry,
and her children's lives are the subject of much of her work, which shows a keen
understanding of the irritations of childhood: the schoolmaster's threatening birch,
the annoyance of tight clothing. However, her lively, witty verse appeals as much to
adults. Married to a Dublin woollen-draper, she was published in England and
admired by poets as well known as Swift and Pope. One of her sons became an eminent
physician, another a miniature-painter.*

from A letter to the Reverend Mr C.

'I pity poor Barber, his wife's so romantic:
A letter in rhyme!—Why, the woman is frantic!
This reading the poets has quite turned her head!
On my life, she should have a dark room and straw bed...
...If ever I marry, I'll choose me a spouse
That shall serve and obey, as she's bound by her vows,
That shall, when I'm dressing, attend like a valet;
Then go to the kitchen, and study my palate.
She has wisdom enough, that keeps out of the dirt,
And can make a good pudding, and cut out a shirt.
What good's in a dame that will pore on a book?
No! Give me the wife that shall save me a cook.'
   Thus far had I written—Then turned to my son,
To give him advice, ere my letter was done.
My son, should you marry, look out for a wife
That's fitted to lighten the labours of life.
Be sure, wed a woman you thoroughly know,
And shun, above all things, a housewifely shrew...
...Avoid the fine lady, whose beauty's her care,
Who sets a high price on her shape, and her air;
Who in dress, and in visits, employs the whole day;
And longs for the evening, to sit down and play.
Choose a woman of wisdom, as well as good breeding,
With a turn, or at least no aversion, to reading:
In the care of her person, exact and refined;
Yet still, let her principal care be her mind...
...When you gain her affection, take care to preserve it
Lest others persuade her, you do not deserve it.
Still study to heighten the joys of her life,
Nor treat her the worse for her being your wife.

If in judgment she errs, set her right without pride:
'Tis the province of insolent fools, to deride.
A husband's first praise, is a Friend and Protector:
Then change not these titles, for Tyrant and Hector...
...So you, in your marriage, shall gain its true end;
And find, in your wife, a Companion and Friend.

CHARLOTTE MEW
1869–1928

The farmer's bride

Three summers since I chose a maid,
Too young maybe—but more's to do
At harvest-time than bide and woo.
   When us was wed she turned afraid
Of love and me and all things human;
Like the shut of a winter's day
Her smile went out, and 'twadn't a woman—
   More like a little frightened fay.
   One night, in the Fall, she runned away.

'Out 'mong the sheep, her be,' they said,
'Should properly have been abed';
But sure enough she wadn't there
Lying awake with her wide brown stare.
So over seven-acre field and up-along across the down
We chased her, flying like a hare
Before our lanterns. To Church-Town
   All in a shiver and a scare
We caught her, fetched her home at last
   And turned the key upon her, fast.

She does the work about the house
As well as most, but like a mouse:
   Happy enough to chat and play
   With birds and rabbits and such as they,
   So long as men-folk keep away.

'Not near, not near!' her eyes beseech
When one of us comes within reach.
   The women say that beasts in stall
   Look round like children at her call.
   I've hardly heard her speak at all.

Shy as a leveret, swift as he,
Straight and slight as a young larch tree,
Sweet as the first wild violets, she,
To her wild self. But what to me?

The short days shorten and the oaks are brown,
   The blue smoke rises to the low grey sky,
One leaf in the still air falls slowly down,
   A magpie's spotted feathers lie
On the black earth spread white with rime,
The berries redden up to Christmas-time.
   What's Christmas-time without there be
   Some other in the house than we!

   She sleeps up in the attic there
   Alone, poor maid. 'Tis but a stair
Betwixt us. Oh! my God! the down,
The soft young down of her, the brown,
The brown of her—her eyes, her hair, her hair!

MOIRA O'NEILL
1864–1955

In 1900 a volume of poems appeared, entitled Songs of the Glens of Antrim, 'written by a Glenswoman in the dialect of the Glens, and chiefly for the pleasure of other Glens-people'. It was a success far beyond this area of Northern Ireland, however, being reissued in 1921 and followed by a further collection in 1922. Its author, writing as 'Moira O'Neill', was Nesta Higginson (later Skrine), who in fact lived not in Ireland but in Canada. Her Collected Poems appeared in 1933.

Her sister

'Brigid is a Caution, sure!'—What's that ye say?
Is it my sister, then, Brigid MacIlray?
Caution or no Caution, listen what I'm telling' ye...
Childer, hould yer noise there, faix! there's no quellin' ye!...
Och, well, I've said it now this many a long day,
'Tis the quare pity o' Brigid MacIlray.

An' she that was the beauty, an' never married yet!
An' fifty years gone over her, but do ye think she'll fret?
Sorra one o' Brigid then, that's not the sort of her,
Ne'er a hate would she care though not a man had thought of her.
Heaps o' men she might 's had... *Here, get out o' that,*
Mick, ye rogue! desthroyin' o' the poor ould cat!

Ah, no use o' talkin'! Sure a woman's born to wed,
An' not go wastin' all her life by waitin' till she's dead.
Haven't we the men to mind, that couldn't for the lives o' them
Keep their right end uppermost, only for the wives o' them?—
Stick to yer pipe, Tim, an' give me no talk now!
There's the door fore'nenst ye, man! out ye can walk now.

Brigid, poor Brigid will never have a child,
An' she you'd think a mother born, so gentle an' so mild...
Danny, is it puttin' little Biddy's eyes out ye're after,
Swishin' wid yer rod there, an' splittin' wid yer laughter?
Come along the whole o' yez, in out o' the wet,
Or may I never but ye'll soon see what ye'll get!

She to have no man at all... *Musha, look at Tim!*
Off an' up the road he is, an' wet enough to swim,
An' his tea sittin' waitin' on him, there he'll sthreel about now,—

Amn't I the heart-scalded woman out an' out now?
Here I've lived an' wrought for him all the ways I can,
But the Goodness grant me patience, for I'd need it wid that man!

What was I sayin' then? Brigid lives her lone,
Ne'er a one about the house, quiet as a stone...
Lave go the pig's tail, boys, an' quet the squealin' now,
Mind! I've got a sally switch that only want the peelin' now...
Ah, just to think of her, 'deed an' well-a-day!
'Tis the quare pity o' Brigid MacIlray.

EVANGELINE PATERSON
Born 1928

Civilisation

Saturday afternoon. Professor Paterson
walks in his garden, bends on his daffodils
looks fond yet stern. His brain, unoccupied, idles.
He hums. Half-heartedly, the watery sun
attempts to gild him, like a saint. He moves
away, deeply ponders a hole in the fence,
reproves a dangling creeper.

     His wife, in the kitchen,
scours the pans. The radio chatters calamity.
Civilisation is teetering to a fall.
Music erupts, with thud and boom and crash
—the mangonels[1] of the last assault? She sluices
water around the sink. She drops a cup.
It shatters.

     Professor Paterson
sits in his usual chair, and reads. Daffodils
stand in a vase behind him. He looks kindly
over his spectacles. The world settles
back on its base.
     Civilisation, it seems,
Is with us yet. She goes to make him tea.

[1] Mangonel = a military engine for casting stones

12 Mother and Child

JUDITH WRIGHT
Born 1915

A fifth generation Australian, Judith travelled round Europe after boarding school and university. She returned to Australia just before World War II. Judith has published ten volumes of poetry, winning the Robert Frost Award in 1975. She is a Christian and an active conservationist, campaigning for forests, wildlife and the Great Barrier Reef.

Woman to man

The eyeless labourer in the night,
the selfless, shapeless seed I hold,
builds for its resurrection day—
silent and swift and deep from sight
foresees the unimagined light.

This is no child with a child's face;
this has no name to name it by:
yet you and I have known it well.
This is our hunter and our chase,
the third who lay in our embrace.

This is the strength that your arm knows,
the arch of flesh that is my breast,
the precise crystals of our eyes.
This is the blood's wild tree that grows
the intricate and folded rose.

This is the maker and the made;
this is the question and reply;
the blind head butting at the dark,
the blaze of light along the blade.
Oh hold me, for I am afraid.

PAULINE STAINER
Born 1941

Pauline read English at St Anne's College, Oxford and took a Master's degree at Southampton University. Her first collection of poems, The Honeycomb, *was published by Bloodaxe Books in 1989 and was a Poetry Book Society recommendation. She lives with her husband and four children in Essex and, as the title of her collection and the end of this poem suggest, they are beekeepers.*

The catalyst

Long after the birth,
she held up the X-ray
of her second-born son
in the womb.

There he hung
against the light,
head-down to the lintel,
translucent
as wax in a glass.

What she saw
was not simply
the curve of the spine,
the seal at the cervix,

but sacrament brightly stilled;
an angelical stone
that cannot be weighed;

the catalyst
of sun through wax—
the ghostly body—
at the casual supper
Christ eating the honeycomb.

ANONYMOUS

Eighteenth century

Until the second half of our own century, a woman who became pregnant outside marriage faced a bleak future. Unless she could marry the child's father, she would become a social outcast, with few means of financial support other than prostitution. To avoid this fate, illegal (and dangerous) abortions were not uncommon. But the emotional, and perhaps physical, agony of the decision is clearly visible behind this somewhat formal poem, with which many women today may still identify.

Epitaph on a child killed by procured abortion

O thou, whose eyes were closed in death's pale night,
Ere fate revealed thee to my aching sight;
Ambiguous something, by no standard fixed,
Frail span, of naught and of existence mixed;
Embryo, imperfect as my torturing thought,
Sad outcast of existence and of naught,
Thou, who to guilty love first ow'st thy frame,
Whom guilty honour kills to hide its shame;
Dire offspring! formed by love's too pleasing power!
Honour's dire victim in a luckless hour!
Soften the pangs that still revenge thy doom:
Nor, from the dark abyss of nature's womb,
Where back I cast thee, let revolving time
Call up past scenes to aggravate my crime.
   Two adverse tyrants ruled thy wayward fate,
Thyself a helpless victim to their hate;
Love, spite of honour's dictates, gave thee breath;
Honour, in spite of love, pronounced thy death.

JOANNA BAILLIE
1762–1851

A mother to her waking infant

Now in thy dazzled, half-oped eye,
Thy curlèd nose and lip awry,
Uphoisted arms and noddling head,
And little chin with crystal spread,
Poor helpless thing! what do I see
That I should sing of thee?

From thy poor tongue no accents come,
Which can but rub thy toothless gum:
Small understanding boasts thy face;
Thy shapeless limbs nor step nor grace:
A few short words thy feats may tell;
And yet I love thee well.

When wakes the sudden bitter shriek,
And redder swells thy little cheek;
When rattled keys thy woes beguile,
And through thine eyelids gleams the smile;
Still for thy weakly self is spent
Thy little silly plaint.

But when thy friends are in distress,
Thou'lt laugh and chuckle ne'ertheless;
Nor with kind sympathy be smitten
Though all are sad but thee and kitten;
Yet, puny varlet as thou art,
Thou twitchest at the heart.

Thy smooth round cheek so soft and warm;
Thy pinky hand and dimpled arm;
Thy silken locks that scantly peep,
With gold-tipp'd ends, where circles deep,
Around thy neck in harmless grace
So soft and sleeky hold their place,
Might harder hearts with kindness fill,
And gain our right good will.

Each passing clown bestows his blessing,
Thy mouth is worn with old wives' kissing:
E'en lighter looks the gloomy eye

Of surly sense when thou art by;
And yet, I think, whoe'er they be,
They love thee not like me.

Perhaps when time shall add a few
Short months to thee, thou'lt love me too;
And after that, through life's long way
Become my sure and cheering stay:
Wilt care for me and be my hold,
When I am weak and old.

Thou'lt listen to my lengthen'd tale,
And pity me when I am frail—
—But see! the sweepy swimming fly,
Upon the window takes thine eye.
Go to thy little senseless play;
Thou dost not heed my lay.

Enigma

O Lord support
all the day long
him whom you have
builded wrong.
Squirrel of the children he
hoarding to himself the map
of his singularity.

Through his half eyes
in thrust back head
what he sees
he has not said.
His squirrel fingers do not well
clutch the things he loves and still
unsprung his tongue his loves to tell.

O Lord a lark
trapped in his breast
that beats
and will not give him rest.
Inside his mouth it beats its wings
and stops his lips and makes him cry
and quivering in him it sings.

Lord, loose the lark
that here is trapped
and trace the maze
that you have mapped.
Squirrel light yet lead with weight
what you mismade do not desert
speak to the inarticulate.

ANN YEARSLEY

1752–1806

Like her mother, Bristol-born Ann Cromartie sold milk from door to door. She married John Yearsley, a labourer, 'of no vice, but very little capacity'. In spite of having six children, she found time to write poetry, never picking up a book till her work was done and the children asleep. The writer and campaigner Hannah More 'discovered' and published her, paying a maid to help with her housework. Sadly, the relationship went sour, as Ann felt manipulated by her 'patroness'. She continued to publish, and ran a library until illness forced her to retire. Her views on child-rearing (below) sound remarkably modern.

from To Mira, on the care of her infant

Mira, as thy dear Edward's senses grow,
Be sure they all will seek this point—to know:
   ...I saw the beauteous Caleb t'other day
Stretch forth his little hand to touch a spray,
Whilst on the grass his drowsy nurse inhaled
The sweets of Nature as her sweets exhaled:
But, ere the infant reached the playful leaf,
She pulled him back—His eyes o'erflowed with grief;
He checked his tears—Her fiercer passions strove,
She looked a vulture cowering o'er a dove!
'I'll teach you, brat!' The pretty trembler sighed—
When, with a cruel shake, she hoarsely cried—
'Your mother spoils you—everything you see
You covet. It shall ne'er be so with me!
Here, eat this cake, sit still, and don't you rise—
Why don't you pluck the sun down from the skies?
I'll spoil your sport—Come, laugh me in the face—
And henceforth learn to keep your proper place.
You rule me in the house!—To hush your noise
I, like a spaniel, must run for toys:
But here, Sir, let the trees alone, nor cry—
Pluck if you dare—Who's master? you, or I?'
   O brutal force, to check th'enquiring mind,
When it would pleasure in a rosebud find!

SUSAN COOLIDGE (SARAH CHAUNCEY WOOLSEY)
1835–1905

Generations of schoolgirls have laughed and cried over What Katy Did *and its sequels, sometimes sentimental but always full of entertaining everyday incidents. Their author was born in Ohio into an academic family (her uncle, brother and nephew were all presidents of Yale). As well as children's books she wrote criticism and edited the letters of Fanny Burney. This poem is Katy's offering at school in the game 'Word and Question', when she has to use the word 'measles' and answer the question 'Who was the grandmother of Invention?'*

Measles

The night it was horribly dark,
The measles broke out in the Ark:
Little Japhet, and Shem, and all the young Hams,
Were screaming at once for potatoes and clams.
And 'What shall I do,' said poor Mrs Noah,
'All alone by myself in this terrible shower?
I know what I'll do: I'll step down in the hold,
And wake up a lioness grim and old,
And tie her close to the children's door,
And give her a ginger-cake to roar
At the top of her voice for an hour or more;
And I'll tell the children to cease their din,
Or I'll let that grim old party in,
To stop their squeazles and likewise their measles.'—
She practised this with the greatest success.
She was everyone's grandmother, I guess.

ROSEMARY DOBSON
Born 1920

Rosemary Dobson, born in Sidney, has published several collections of verse and compiled anthologies, including two books of poems translated from the Russian. She won the Robert Frost Award in 1979. She lives in Canberra.

Cock crow

Wanting to be myself, alone,
Between the lit house and the town
I took the road, and at the bridge
Turned back and walked the way I'd come.

Three times I took that lonely stretch,
Three times the dark trees closed me round,
The night absolved me of my bonds
Only my footsteps held the ground.

My mother and my daughter slept,
One life behind and one before,
And I that stood between denied
Their needs in shutting-to the door.

And walking up and down the road
Knew myself, separate and alone,
Cut off from human cries, from pain,
And love that grows about the bone.

Too brief illusion! Thrice for me
I heard the cock crow on the hill,
And turned the handle of the door
Thinking I knew his meaning well.

KATHARINE TYNAN HINKSON
1861–1931

A leading figure in the Irish Celtic Revival, Katharine was a close friend of Alice Meynell and is buried next to her in London. A County Dublin farmer's daughter and a Roman Catholic, she was convent-educated (she would stuff forbidden reading inside her bodice to hide it from the nuns!). Katharine married Henry Albert Hinkson, a lawyer, and they lived first in London and later in Mayo. She wrote over a hundred novels, a series of autobiographical works and several collections of poems.

The childless woman in heaven

The children she had missed,
That never yet had birth,
Unwarmed, unfed, unkissed,
Soured all her joy on earth.

But when her day was done
And none were desolate,
Dusty and all alone,
She knocked at Heaven's gate.

Birds from a parapet
Called to her clear and shrill;
With 'Mother! Mother!' so wild and sweet,
And they were never still.

They were no birds at all,
But children small and bright;
When she came past the high wall
They were as birds in flight.

One was clasping her hand;
One was hugging her gown;
The littlest one of all the band
She lifted nor set him down.

Her hungry heart and cold
Was filled full and to spare:
One had her feet to hold,
One was kissing her hair.

The heart in her side
Forgot the ancient wrong:
When 'Mother! Mother! Mother!' they cried,
It soared like a bird's song.

Her arms were full of children,
As they were in the nest.
The littlest one crept softly in,
So he lay in her breast.

God's people passing by,
They smiled at her heart's ease;
'The mother of many children,
Her flowers grown to her knees.'

They dance, they laugh, they run,
She laughs with them at play;
Their pleasures are not done
Nor their sweet holiday.

When they lie down at night,
Soft pillows, downiest beds,
Her arms are full of her birds bright,
Dark heads and golden heads.

She draws them close to her,
Lest haply it should seem
That the new life in some wild fear
Was a dream, but a dream.

JENNY ROBERTSON
Born 1942

*A Glasgow childhood and the experience of working with displaced persons in
northern Germany made Jenny Robertson take up social work. However, when caring
for her children and her elderly mother kept her at home, she returned to her first love
of writing. As well as novels for children and young people and a play, she has
published two collections of poems,* Beyond the Border *and* Ghetto, *a poetic
exploration of the experience of the Warsaw Ghetto. She and her husband Stuart have
travelled regularly to Eastern Europe to support Christians there. Much of her work is
informed by her faith, her concern for justice and for women's status.*

Three a.m.—a mother waits

Nuns keep vigil with psalm and measured voice;
nurses manoeuvre amidst moans and snores.
Rocked against the long-drawn ticking night,
dry-mouthed, driven from sleep, I wait,
imagine in each bang and engine noise
the overdue return, the rasping key.
Get up, grope for his empty bed and pray
no less devoutly than devoted soeurs,
as anxiously as nurses watch for day.
Morning is now four short hours away.
The wind blows litter over silent streets.
Dossers and drunks find huddled brief respite
and junkies dream gaunt nightmares. My fears
fuse with relief and fury—the boy appears.

EVANGELINE PATERSON
Born 1928

A wish for my children

On this doorstep I stand
year after year
and watch you leaving

and think: May you not
skin your knees. May you
not catch your fingers
in car doors. May
your hearts not break.

May tide and weather
wait for your coming

and may you grow strong
to break
all webs of my weaving.

13 Friends and Foes

ANNE FINCH
1661–1720

Friendship between Ephelia and Ardelia

Ephelia: What Friendship is, Ardelia, show.

Ardelia: 'Tis to love, as I love you.

E: This account, so short (though kind),
Suits not my enquiring mind.
Therefore farther now repeat:
What is Friendship when complete?

A: 'Tis to share all joy and grief;
'Tis to lend all due relief
From the tongue, the heart, the hand;
'Tis to mortgage house and land;
For a friend be sold a slave;
'Tis to die upon a grave,
If a friend therein do lie.

E: This indeed, though carried high;
This, though more than e'er was done
Underneath the rolling sun,
This has all been said before.
Can Ardelia say no more?

A: Words indeed no more can show:
But 'tis to love, as I love you.

MATILDA BETHAM
1776–1852

'In our quiet and unorganized household...learning unlocked her abstruse stores and people talked...as if in the house of a philosopher.' Thus Matilda, eldest of fourteen children of a Herefordshire rector, described her childhood. Later she supported herself by miniature painting and writing, which included a biographical dictionary of famous women. Disappointed in her longing to marry, she suffered a breakdown but later recovered and settled in London where she had many literary friends.

In a letter to A. R. C. on her wishing to be called Anna

Forgive me, if I wound your ear
    By calling of you Nancy
Which is the name of my sweet friend,
    The other's but her fancy.

Ah, dearest girl! how could your mind
    The strange distinction frame?
The whimsical, unjust caprice,
    Which robs you of your name.

Nancy agrees with what we see,
    A being wild and airy;
Gay as a nymph of Flora's train,
    Fantastic as a fairy.

But Anna's of a different kind,
    A melancholy maid;
Boasting a sentimental soul,
    In solemn pomp arrayed.

Oh ne'er will I forsake the sound,
    So artless and so free!
Be what you will with all mankind,
    But Nancy still with me.

Rossetti's strange fantasy Goblin market *tells how Lizzie, by tasting the magical goblin fruits, rescues her sister Laura from the death they bring. This extract is the poem's ending.*

from Goblin market

That night long Lizzie watched by her,
Counted her pulse's flagging stir,
Felt for her breath,

Held water to her lips, and cooled her face
With tears and fanning leaves:
But when the first birds chirped about their eaves,
And early reapers plodded to the place
Of golden sheaves,

And dew-wet grass
Bowed in the morning winds so brisk to pass,
And new buds with new day
Opened of cup-like lilies on the stream,
Laura awoke as from a dream,
Laughed in the innocent old way,
Hugged Lizzie but not twice or thrice;
Her gleaming locks showed not one thread of grey,
Her breath was sweet as May
And light danced in her eyes.

Days, weeks, months, years
Afterwards, when both were wives
With children of their own;
Their mother-hearts beset with fear,
Their lives bound up in tender lives;
Laura would call the little ones
And tell them of their early prime,

Those pleasant days long gone
Of not-returning time:
Would talk about the haunted glen,
The wicked, quaint fruit-merchant men,
Their fruits like honey to the throat
But poison in the blood;

(Men sell not such in any town:)
Would tell them how her sister stood
In deadly peril to do her good,
And win the fiery antidote:
Then joining hands to little hands
Would bid them cling together,
'For there is no friend like a sister
In calm or stormy weather;
To cheer one on the tedious way,
To fetch one if one goes astray,
To lift one if one totters down,
To strengthen whilst one stands.'

ADELAIDE PROCTER
1825–64

*Many still know the popular Victorian song 'The Lost Chord'; fewer know its author's
other works. Adelaide, Queen Victoria's favourite poet, was the daughter of another
poet, Bryan Procter (who wrote as Barry Cornwall). Much of her work was first
published in* Household Words *and other magazines, and her collected poems went
through many editions. She also wrote many hymns. She became a Roman Catholic in
1851 and took an active interest in the social conditions of women.*

Envy

He was the first always: Fortune
   Shone bright in his face.
I fought for years; with no effort
   He conquered the place:
We ran; my feet were all bleeding,
   But he won the race.

Spite of his many successes
   Men loved him the same;
My one pale ray of good fortune
   Met scoffing and blame.
When we erred, they gave him pity,
   But me—only shame.

My home was still in the shadow,
   His lay in the sun:
I longed in vain: what he asked for
   It straightway was done.
Once I staked all my heart's treasure,
   We played—and he won.

Yes; and just now I have seen him,
   Cold, smiling, and blest,
Laid in his coffin. God help me!
   While he is at rest,
I am cursed still to live:—even
   Death loved him the best.

ELIZABETH WORDSWORTH
1840–1932

To today's students of Lady Margaret Hall, Oxford, 'Wordsworth' is a hall of residence, but to the first students of the then women's college, Elizabeth Wordsworth was its pioneering Principal. For thirty years her life centred on the college, as she built up its membership from nine to fifty-nine. Grand-niece of William Wordsworth and daughter of the headmaster of Harrow, she also founded St Hugh's College. Elizabeth wrote essays, poems, plays and a biography of her father. She received two honorary higher degrees and was made a Dame Commander of the British Empire.

Good and clever

If all the good people were clever,
    And all clever people were good,
The world would be nicer than ever
    We thought that it possibly could.

But somehow 'tis seldom or never
    The two hit it off as they should,
The good are so harsh to the clever,
    The clever, so rude to the good!

So friends, let it be our endeavour
    To make each by each understood;
For few can be good, like the clever,
    Or clever, so well as the good.

A garland of precepts

Though a seeker since my birth,
Here is all I've learned on earth,
This is the gist of all I know:
Give advice and buy a foe.
Random truths are all I find
Stuck like burrs about my mind.
Salve a blister. Burn a letter.
Do not wash a cashmere sweater.
Tell a tale but seldom twice.
Give a stone before advice.

Pressed for rules and verities,
All I recollect are these:
Feed a cold and starve a fever.
Argue with no true believer.
Think-too-long is never act.
Scratch a myth and find a fact.
Stitch in time saves twenty stitches.
Give the rich, to please them, riches.
Give to love your hearth and hall,
But do not give advice at all.

14 Justice

KATHERINE PHILIPS
1631–64

Upon the double murther of King Charles I

I think not on the State, nor am concerned
Which way soever the great helm is turned:
But as that son, whose father's danger nigh
Did force his native dumbness, and untie
The fettered organs—so this is a cause
That will excuse the breach of Nature's laws.
Silence were now a sin; nay, passion now
Wise men themselves for merit would allow!
What noble eye could see, and careless, pass,
The dying lion kicked by every ass?
Has Charles so broke God's laws he must not have
A quiet crown, nor yet a quiet grave?
Tombs have been sanctuaries, thieves lie there
Secure from all their penalty and fear.
Great Charles his double misery was this:
Unfaithful friends, ignoble enemies.
Had any heathen been this Prince's foe,
He would have wept to see him injured so.
His title was his crime; they'd reason good
To quarrel at the right they had withstood.
'He broke God's laws, and therefore he must die'?
And what shall then become of you and I?
Slander must follow treason; but yet, stay!
Take not our reason with our King away.
Though you have seized upon all our defence,
Yet do not sequester our common sense.
'Christ will be King'? but I ne'er understood
His subjects built His Kingdom up with blood,
Except their own; or that He would dispense
With His commands, though for His own defence.
O to what height of horror are they come
Who dare pull down a crown, tear up a tomb!

SOJOURNER TRUTH
1797–1883

In 1827 the New York Emancipation Act allowed Isabella, a slave, to gain her freedom. In 1843 she set out with 25 cents and a bag of clothes and, taking the name Sojourner Truth, she travelled the coast singing and speaking on slavery and women's rights. Tall, witty and dramatic, she fascinated white audiences. But her petition on black land ownership, the work of years, gathered dust on a Congress shelf. This famous speech has been set out as poetry by Erlene Stetson.

Ain't I a woman?

That man over there say
   a woman needs to be helped into carriages
and lifted over ditches
   and to have the best place everywhere.
Nobody ever helped me into carriages
   or over mud puddles
     or gives me a best place...

And ain't I a woman?
   Look at me
Look at my arm!
   I have plowed and planted
and gathered into barns
   and no man could head me...
And ain't I a woman?
   I could work as much
and eat as much as a man—
   when I could get to it—
and bear the lash as well
   and ain't I a woman?
I have born thirteen children
   and seen most all sold into slavery
and when I cried out a mother's grief
   none but Jesus heard me...
and ain't I a woman?
   that little man in black there say
a woman can't have as much rights as a man
   cause Christ wasn't a woman
Where did your Christ come from?
   From God and a woman!
Man had nothing to do with him!

If the first woman God ever made
was strong enough to turn the world
upside down, all alone
together women ought to be able to turn it
rightside up again.

JULIA WARD HOWE
1819–1910

Hymns by nineteenth-century women still form a major part of Christian worship, but none have entered a nation's consciousness so thoroughly as Julia Ward Howe's stirring 'Battle Hymn' for the northern states in the American Civil War. Daughter of a New York banker, Julia married the anti-slavery campaigner Samuel Howe, twenty years her senior. She joined a Boston literary circle and wrote a play and two travel books as well as many poems.

Battle Hymn of the Republic

Mine eyes have seen the glory of the coming of the Lord:
He is trampling out the vintage where the grapes of wrath are stored;
He has loosed the fatal lightning of his terrible swift sword:
　　His truth is marching on.

I have seen him in the watch-fires of a hundred circling camps;
They have builded him an altar in the evening dews and damps;
I can read his righteous sentence by the dim and flaring lamps:
　　His day is marching on.

I have read a fiery gospel, writ in burnish'd rows of steel:
'As ye deal with my contemners, so with you my grace shall deal;
Let the Hero, born of woman, crush the serpent with his heel!
　　Since God is marching on.'

He has sounded forth the trumpet that shall never call retreat;
He is sifting out the hearts of men before his Judgment Seat;
O, be swift, my soul, to answer Him, be jubilant, my feet!
　　Our God is marching on.

In the beauty of the lilies Christ was born, across the sea,
With a glory in His bosom that transfigures you and me:
As He died to make men holy, let us die to make men free,
　　While God is marching on.

FRANCES HARPER
1825–1911

Born in Maryland and orphaned at three, Frances was brought up by an uncle and went to the school he ran for free black people. She lectured against slavery and, after the Civil War, on the need to educate former slaves. She published many poems including some on biblical themes connected with liberation, such as the story of Moses.

A double standard

Do you blame me that I loved him?
    If when standing all alone
I cried for bread, a careless world
    Pressed to my lips a stone?

Do you blame me that I loved him,
    That my heart beat glad and free,
When he told me in the sweetest tones
    He loved but only me?

Can you blame me that I did not see,
    Beneath his burning kiss,
The serpent's wiles, nor even less hear
    The deadly adder hiss?

Can you blame me that my heart grew cold,
    That the tempted tempter turned—
When he was feted and caressed
    And I was coldly spurned?

Would you blame him, when you drew from me
    Your dainty robes aside,
If he with gilded baits should claim
    Your fairest as his bride?

Would you blame the world if it should press
    On him a civic crown;
And see me struggling in the depth,
    Then harshly press me down?

Can you blame me if I've learned to think
    Your hate of vice a sham,
When you so coldly crushed me down,
    And then excused the man?

Yes, blame me for my downward course,
    But oh! remember well,
Within your homes you press the hand
    That led me down to hell!

I'm glad God's ways are not your ways,
    He does not see as man;
Within His love I know there's room
    For those whom others ban.

I think before his great white throne,
    His throne of spotless light,
That whited sepulchres shall wear
    The hue of endless night.

That I who fell, and he who sinned,
    Shall reap as we have sown;
That each the burden of his loss
    Must bear, and bear alone.

No golden weights can turn the scale
    Of justice in His sight;
And what is wrong in woman's life
    In man's cannot be right.

MARY COLERIDGE
1861–1907

An insincere wish addressed to a beggar

We are not near enough to love,
   I can but pity all your woe;
For wealth has lifted me above,
   And falsehood set you down below.

If you were true, we still might be
   Brothers in something more than name;
And were I poor, your love to me
   Would make our differing bonds the same.

But golden gates between us stretch,
   Truth opens her forbidding eyes;
You can't forget that I am rich,
   Nor I that you are telling lies.

Love never comes but at love's call,
   And pity asks for him in vain;
Because I cannot give you all,
   You give me nothing back again.

And you are right with all your wrong,
   For less than all is nothing too;
May Heaven beggar me ere long,
   And Truth reveal herself to you!

JOY DAVIDMAN
1915–1960

'Here is what an intelligent, sensitive and vivid mind thinks about itself and the things of the modern world,' said a critic of Joy's 1938 collection Letter to a Comrade, *which shared an American poetry prize with Robert Frost. A Jewish atheist and a Communist, in this poem she responds to the horrors of the Spanish Civil War. After failing as a teacher and a Hollywood scriptwriter she became a film reviewer. An unhappy marriage with the alcoholic Bill Gresham (by whom she had two sons), and her correspondence with C.S.Lewis, led to her conversion to Christianity. In 1956 Lewis, 'confirmed bachelor', married Joy to give her British residence rights, but when she fell ill with cancer he realized that he loved her. After a miraculous remission of the disease they enjoyed a few years of great happiness. Lewis recorded his devastation at her death in* A Grief Observed.

Snow in Madrid

Softly, so casual,
Lovely, so light, so light,
The cruel sky lets fall
Something one does not fight.

How tenderly to crown
The brutal year
The clouds send something down
That one need not fear.

Men before perishing
See with unwounded eye
For once a gentle thing
Fall from the sky.

PART THREE

Her Faith

'What women these Christians have!' exclaimed an observer of the early
church.

Christianity has not always lived up to its own declaration that 'in Christ
there is neither male nor female'. Even so, women have always formed a
large part of the church's membership, and found in Jesus a Saviour who
gave their lives meaning and worth. Whenever the winds of freedom and
revival have blown through the churches, pioneering women have been at
the forefront of change.

Are women 'naturally' more religious than men? Some have thought so.
This section suggests rather that women have particular perspectives on
faith. In their vulnerability they can understand the Christ who becomes a
helpless baby, and opens himself to the risk of the cross. Used to dealing
with everyday realities, they often have a down-to-earth, unpretentious
approach to faith. Perhaps women are also more able than men to 'be in
two places at once': sweeping the house, and at the same time caught up in a
vision of the Creator.

In this part of the anthology we see poets glimpsing God in the natural
world and in the details of daily life; searching for a relationship with that
God; meeting God in the life, death and resurrection of Jesus. We join them
as they celebrate the times when God's love breaks through, and as they
wrestle with the times when God seems absent. Sometimes they hang on to
faith only by the skin of their teeth—but perhaps that is when faith is
strongest. And we end with a burst of praise for the God who made us, and
gave us words to praise with.

15 God in her world

ANNE FINCH
1661–1720

The atheist and the acorn

'Methinks this world is oddly made,
   And everything's amiss,'
A dull presuming atheist said,
As stretched he lay beneath a shade,
   And instancèd in this:

'Behold,' quoth he, 'that mighty thing,
   A pumpkin, large and round,
Is held but by a little string,
Which upwards cannot make it spring,
   Or bear it from the ground;

'Whilst on this oak, a fruit so small,
   So disproportioned, grows;
That, who with sense surveys this All,
This universal casual ball,
   Its ill contrivance knows.

'My better judgment would have hung
   That weight upon a tree,
And left this mast, thus slightly strung,
'Mongst things which on the surface sprung,
   And small and feeble be.'

No more the caviller could say,
   Nor farther faults descry;
For, as he upwards gazing lay,
An acorn loosened from the stay
   Fell down upon his eye.

The offended part with tears ran o'er,
   As punished for the sin;
Fool! had that bough a pumpkin bore,
Thy whimsies must have worked no more,
   Nor skull had kept them in.

HANNAH MORE
1745–1833

Jacob More, Master of the Free School of Fishponds, near Bristol, trained his five daughters from an early age to earn their living as teachers. Hannah, the fourth, taught at the successful school which her three elder sisters ran. Given an annuity by her former fiancé, who broke off the engagement, she was able to give time to writing prose, plays and poetry on moral and educational topics, and religious tracts. She was active in promoting Sunday schools. A visitor described the home she shared with her sisters as 'the seat of piety, cheerfulness, literature and hospitality'.

from Patient Joe, or the Newcastle collier

It was Joseph's ill-fortune to work in a pit
With some who believed that profaneness was wit;
When disasters befell him much pleasure they showed,
And laughed and said—'Joseph, will this work for good?'

But ever when these would profanely advance
That this happened by luck, and that happened by chance,
Still Joseph insisted no chance could be found,
Not a sparrow by accident falls to the ground.

Among his companions who worked in the pit,
And made him the butt of their profligate wit,
Was idle Tim Jenkins, who drank and who gamed,
Who mocked at his Bible, and was not ashamed.

One day at the pit his old comrades he found,
And they chatted, preparing to go under ground;
Tim Jenkins as usual was turning to jest
Joe's notion—that all things which happened were best.

As Joe on the ground had unthinkingly laid
His provision for dinner of bacon and bread,
A dog on the watch seized the bread and the meat,
And off with his prey ran with footsteps so fleet.

Now to see the delight that Tim Jenkins expressed!
'Is the loss of thy dinner too, Joe, for the best?'
'No doubt on't,' said Joe, 'but as I must eat,
'Tis my duty to try to recover my meat.'

So saying he followed the dog a long round,
While Tim, laughing and swearing, went down under ground.
Poor Joe soon returned, though his bacon was lost,
For the dog a good dinner had made at his cost.

When Joseph came back, he expected a sneer,
But the face of each collier spoke horror and fear;
'What a narrow escape hast thou had,' they all said,
'The pit is fall'n in, and Tim Jenkins is dead!'

How sincere was the gratitude Joseph expressed!
How warm the compassion which glowed in his breast!
Thus events great and small, if aright understood,
Will be found to be working together for good.

'When my meat,' Joseph cried, 'was just now stol'n away,
And I had no prospect of eating today,
How could it appear to a short-sighted sinner,
That my life would be saved by the loss of my dinner?'

ELIZABETH BARRETT BROWNING
1806–61

The best

What's the best thing in the world?
June-rose, by May-dew impearl'd;
Sweet south-wind, that means no rain;
Truth, not cruel to a friend;
Pleasure, not in haste to end;
Beauty, not self-deck'd and curl'd
Till its pride is over-plain;
Light, that never makes you wink;
Memory, that gives no pain;
Love, when, so, you're loved again.
What's the best thing in the world?
—Something out of it, I think.

EMILY BRONTË
1818–48

Last lines

No coward soul is mine,
No trembler in the world's storm-troubled sphere:
   I see Heaven's glories shine,
And faith shines equal, arming me from fear.

   O God within my breast,
Almighty, ever-present Deity!
   Life—that in me has rest,
As I—undying Life—have power in Thee!

   Vain are the thousand creeds
That move men's hearts: unutterably vain;
   Worthless as wither'd weeds,
Or idlest froth amid the boundless main,

   To waken doubt in one
Holding so fast by Thine infinity;
   So surely anchor'd on
The steadfast rock of immortality.

   With wide-embracing love
Thy Spirit animates eternal years,
   Pervades and broods above,
Changes, sustains, dissolves, creates, and rears.

   Though earth and man were gone,
And suns and universes cease to be,
   And Thou were left alone,
Every existence would exist in Thee.

   There is not room for Death,
Nor atom that his might could render void:
   Thou—Thou art Being and Breath,
And what Thou art may never be destroyed.

EMILY DICKINSON
1830–84

The only news I know

The only news I know
Is bulletins all day
From immortality;

The only shows I see
Tomorrow and today,
Perchance eternity.

The only one I meet
Is God, the only street
Existence; this traversed,

If other news there be
Or admirabler show,
I'll tell it you.

KATHARINE TYNAN HINKSON
1861–1931

Of an orchard

Good is an Orchard, the Saint saith,
To meditate on life and death,
With a cool well, a hive of bees,
A hermit's grot below the trees.

Good is an Orchard: very good,
Though one should wear no monkish hood;
Right good when Spring awakes her flute,
And good in yellowing time of fruit:

Very good in the grass to lie
And see the network 'gainst the sky,
A living lace of blue and green
And boughs that let the gold between.

The bees are types of souls that dwell
With honey in a quiet cell;
The ripe fruit figures goldenly
The soul's perfection in God's eye.

Prayer and praise in a country home
Honey and fruit: a man might come
Fed on such meats to walk abroad
And in his Orchard talk with God.

LUCI SHAW
Born 1928

Luci grew up in England, Australia and Canada, studied at Wheaton College, USA and married an American, Harold Shaw, with whom she ran a publishing firm. Until Harold's death they lived in Illinois 'on an acre of oaks and black walnuts'. She now divides her time between Illinois and the West Coast, and lectures at colleges and workshops on poetry and creativity. She has published five collections of poems and a book on her bereavement. Luci has five grown-up children.

Circles

I sing of circles, rounded things,
    apples and wreaths and wedding rings,
and domes and spheres,
      and falling tears,
well-rounded meals,
      water wheels,
bottoms of bells,
    or walled-in wells;
rain dropping, golden in the air
    or silver on your shining hair;
pebbles in pewter-coloured ponds
    making circles, rounds on rounds;
the curve of a repeating rhyme;
    the circle of the face of time.
Beyond these circles I can see
    the circle of eternity.

Does passing of each season fair
    make of the four a noble square?
No. For to each the others lend
    a cyclic, curving, rhythmic blend.
Remember, spring in summer gone
    comes round again. New spring comes on.

The circle in the eagle's eye
mirrors the circle of the sky,
the blue horizon, end to end,
end to end,
over earth's never-ending bend.

The arc of love from God to men
orbiting, goes to him again.
My love, to loving God above,
captures *me* in the round of love.

16 God with her

MADELEINE L'ENGLE
Born 1919

When Madeleine met a sudden writer's block after five novels, she and her actor husband, Hugh, ran the general store in their Connecticut town to survive. Even when she began to write again, her children's fantasy A Wrinkle in Time struggled to find a publisher. But it was published—and won the Newbery Medal. Other awards followed as Madeleine produced more of her strange, gripping books. A former atheist whose Christian faith is now deepened by new trends in science, she is librarian and writer-in-residence at the Cathedral of St John the Divine, New York.

O Sapientia

It was from Joseph first I learned
Of love. Like me he was dismayed.
How easily he could have turned
Me from his house; but, unafraid,
He put me not away from him
(O God-sent angel, pray for him).
Thus through his love was Love obeyed.

The Child's first cry came like a bell:
God's word aloud, God's word in deed.
The angel spoke: so it befell,
And Joseph with me in my need.
O Child whose father came from heaven,
To you another gift was given,
Your earthly father chosen well.

With Joseph I was always warmed
And cherished. Even in the stable
I knew that I would not be harmed.
And, though above the angels swarmed,
Man's love it was that made me able
To bear God's love, wild, formidable,
To bear God's will, through me performed.

SUSAN MITCHELL

1866–1926

Aids to the Immortality of Certain Persons in Ireland, Charitably Administered by Susan Mitchell *was Susan's first poetry collection, which gently satirized some literary and public figures of 1908. Two more volumes of religious verse followed from this County Leitrim bank manager's daughter, who mixed in Irish literary circles (she stayed with Yeats while undergoing treatment for deafness in London). Susan contributed essays and criticism to Irish journals and was known as 'a generous, kind and witty hostess'.*

The star of the heart

The star has risen in the heart,
The sweet light flushes every part.
The shepherds of the body know,
The rumour reached them long ago,
Abiding in the fields were they
When deity informed the clay.
The wise kings of the mind bow down,
They yield the wiser king his crown;
Before a cradle they unfold
The myrrh and frankincense and gold.

JANET LEWIS
Born 1899

Best known as a novelist, Janet Lewis has also written children's books and opera librettos. She is American, and has taught writing at various universities in the United States.

A lullaby

Lullee, lullay,
I could not love thee more
If thou wast Christ the King.
Now tell me, how did Mary know
That in her womb should sleep and grow
The Lord of everything?

Lullee, lullay,
An angel stood with her
Who said, 'That which doth stir
Like summer in thy side
Shall save the world from sin.
Then stable, hall and inn
Shall cherish Christmas-tide.'

Lullee, lullay,
And so it was that Day.
And did she love Him more
Because an angel came
To prophesy His name?
Ah no, not so,
She could not love Him more,
But loved Him just the same.
Lullee, lullee, lullay.

ELIZABETH ROONEY
Born 1924

Although her first degree was in English, Elizabeth did not begin writing poetry until 1978, after joining the Society of the Companions of the Holy Cross, an order of Episcopal lay women. She is married to an Episcopal priest and they have two sons and two daughters. Now both retired, the Rooneys live in the house where Elizabeth grew up, on a farm in Wisconsin. Under the farm is a limestone cavern, the Cave of the Mounds, which is run as a tourist attraction.

Creator

Jesus, Jesus,
Carpenter of Nazareth,
Can you make a lintel?
Can you make a door?

Jesus, Jesus,
Carpenter of Nazareth,
Can you make a universe
Where there was none before?

Jesus, Jesus,
Carpenter of Nazareth,
Living in the midst of us,
A working man and poor,

How shall we esteem you,
Holy, humble carpenter?
By the universe you made—
And also by the door.

VERONICA ZUNDEL
Born 1953

A quiet roar

one
he lays his left hand along the beam
hand that moulded clay into fluttering birds
hand that cupped wild flowers to learn their peace
hand that stroked the bee's soft back and touched death's sting

two
he stretches his right hand across the grain
hand that blessed a dead corpse quick
hand that smeared blind spittle into sight
hand that burgeoned bread, smoothed down the rumpled sea

three
he stands laborious
sagging, split,
homo erectus, poor bare forked thing
hung on nails like a picture

he is not beautiful
blood sweats from him in rain

far off where we are lost, desert dry
thunder begins its quiet roar
the first drops startle us alive
the cloud no bigger
than a man's hand

MAY PROBYN
Nineteenth century

*A few collections of devotional verse and some children's stories by May Probyn
appeared between 1878 and 1895. She seems then to have disappeared from history.
But the powerful challenge of this poem, chosen by Arthur Quiller-Couch in his 1912
Oxford Book of Victorian Verse, lives on.*

Is it nothing to you?

We were playing on the green together,
　　My sweetheart and I—
O! so heedless in the gay June weather
　　When the word went forth that we must die.
O! so merrily the balls of amber
　　And of ivory we tossed to the sky,
While the word went forth in the King's chamber
　　That we both must die.

O! so idly straying thro' the pleasaunce
　　Pluck'd we here and there
Fruit and bud, while in the royal presence
　　The King's son was casting from his hair
Glory of the wreathen gold that crown'd it,
　　And, ungirdling all his garments fair,
Flinging by the jewell'd clasp that bound it,
　　With his feet made bare.

Down the myrtled stairway of the palace,
　　Ashes on his head,
Came he, thro' the rose and citron alleys,
　　In rough sark of sackcloth habited,
And in the hempen halter—O! we jested
　　Lightly, and we laugh'd as he was led
To the torture, while the bloom we breasted
　　Where the grapes grew red.

O! so sweet the bird, when he was dying,
　　Piped to her and me—
Is no room this glad June day for sighing—
　　He is dead, and she and I go free!
When the sun shall set on all our pleasure
　　We will mourn him—What, so you decree
We are heartless? Nay, but in what measure
　　Do you more than we?

ISOBEL THRILLING
Contemporary

Isobel first began writing after a series of eye operations which saved her sight. Her poetry collection Ultrasonics of Snow *was published in 1985, and another collection is forthcoming. She has had poems broadcast on radio and television and published in magazines and anthologies.*

Before Easter

Spring;
yet frost still builds
dead palaces.

We hear the crack from
icicles of bone,
snow crowns
have snapped the throats
of daffodils,
the ice-queen walks in
her brittle dress.

No rose-blood in the stem,
no cumulus
perfume in trees,
each day
is a coffin of glass.

The sun is turned
to crystal,
it is our alchemy of winter;
inner cold.

Christ sleeps
behind the quickening stone.

MARION PITMAN
Born 1955

Easter midnight service

A pagan fire to conjure in the spring—
But this fire we have lit to conjure out
The winter chill of all the pagan rout,
And conjure in the summer of the king.
Soon will the brazen bells of triumph ring,
And midnight dark be shaken by a shout
That death's cold chain that gripped the world about
Is broken link from link: and the links sing.

And fire from fire our candles take the light,
As we take fire from the eternal flame,
And flame from flame we walk down the dark aisle,
Each flame a glory gold against the night,
That trembles at the whisper of the name
That burns through all the empty halls of hell.

When Mary thro' the garden went

When Mary thro' the garden went,
　　There was no sound of any bird,
And yet, because the night was spent,
　　The little grasses lightly stirred,
　　The flowers awoke, the lilies heard.

When Mary thro' the garden went,
　　The dew lay still on flower and grass,
The waving palms above her sent
　　Their fragrance out as she did pass,
　　No light upon the branches was.

When Mary thro' the garden went,
　　Her eyes, for weeping long, were dim,
The grass beneath her footsteps bent,
　　The solemn lilies, white and slim,
　　These also stood and wept for Him.

When Mary thro' the garden went,
　　She sought, within the garden ground,
One for Whom her heart was rent,
　　One Who for her sake was bound,
　　One Who sought and she was found.

ALICE MEYNELL
1847–1922

Christ in the universe

With this ambiguous earth
His dealings have been told us. These abide:
The signal to a maid, the human birth,
The lesson, and the young Man crucified.

But not a star of all
The innumerable host of stars has heard
How he administered this terrestrial ball.
Our race have kept their Lord's entrusted Word.

Of his earth-visiting feet
None knows the secret, cherished, perilous,
The terrible, shamefast, frightened, whispered, sweet
Heart-shattering secret of His way with us.

No planet knows that this
Our wayside planet, carrying land and wave,
Love and life multiplied, and pain and bliss,
Bears, as chief treasure, one forsaken grave.

Nor, in our little day,
May his devices with the heavens be guessed,
His pilgrimage to thread the Milky Way,
Or his bestowals there be manifest.

But, in the eternities,
Doubtless we shall compare together, hear
A million alien Gospels, in what guise
He trod the Pleiades, the Lyre, the Bear.

O be prepared, my soul!
To read the inconceivable, to scan
The million forms of God those stars unroll
When, in our turn, we show to them a Man.

'It is not God's will for any to be lost, but for all to come to repentance,' said St Peter in his second letter. Anne, rejecting the 'hell-fire' preaching of her day, nurtured the same desire; believing firmly that there was no way to God but through Jesus, she longed that all should finally accept that way. Some may think her poem heretical; many others will welcome this heartfelt cry of a sensitive soul.

A hope

And oh! there lives within my heart
    A hope, long nursed by me;
(And should its cheering ray depart
    How dark my soul would be!)

That as in Adam all have died,
    In Christ shall all men live;
And ever round His throne abide,
    Eternal praise to give.

That even the wicked shall at last
    Be fitted for the skies;
And when their dreadful doom is past
    To light and life arise.

I ask not how remote the day,
    Nor what the sinners' woe,
Before their dross is purged away;
    Enough for me to know—

That when the cup of wrath is drained,
    The metal purified,
They'll cling to what they once disdained,
    And live by Him that died.

17 Her Faith's Journey

HANNAH WALLIS
Eighteenth century

'This poor Methodist will never write tolerable verse,' concluded the Monthly Review *in 1789 on receiving Hannah's book* The Female's Meditations; Or, Common Occurrences Spiritualised. *Hannah grew up in an Essex village and by 1787, when the book appeared, she was elderly and had lost her father (who collapsed in Chelmsford Market), her mother, sister and brother. This may explain her rather morbid dwelling on death; but there is an engaging directness in the simple, sometimes ungrammatical language and sincere faith of her poems.*

To a sick friend

Dear girl, you're growing very thin,
    Your roses too are fled;
You say you are low-spirited,
    And death you seem to dread.

Why do you dread this cruel foe?
    He's only so through sin:
Be careful to examine oft
    The state your soul is in.

Is it the terror of the law
    Does on your spirits prey?
I know you strictly was brought up
    In a religious way.

But as you did in Adam fall,
    So must a sinner be;
My dear, you must be born again—
    Look in God's word, and see.

If you've experienced such a change,
    You'll love the Saviour dear;
Then happier you will be in death,
    Than longer living here.

LESLEY DICKENS
Born 1963

This poem, included in the 1989 poetry competition anthology of the Fellowship of Christian Writers, is Lesley's first nationally published poem. Her career has been steadily moving in a literary direction: after taking sciences at school and working for several years as an auditor in the public sector, she studied English Literature at evening classes and is now working towards an English degree at Manchester University.

The fence

The framework was founded
before I acknowledged a boundary
but when I saw its bare structure
its feet deeply trenched, its arms

inviting cover; I began to gather
wooden slats, to shape and smooth,
to measure and to count the length.
I did not question. A fence is a fence.

I knew the carpenter's joy,
the pleasure and the pain of wood;
the smooth face of work well done
the bloodied broken hands

I understood. A fence is a fence.
No pretence. It separates, divides,
fulfils a territorial need, sets
out the space in which to live our lives.

The gap grew smaller till I could
no longer pass from side to side
though still could reach your hand
should your heart dare the crossing.

Without a question. I raised the last
plank, set it to bridge a space
took up the Roman nail, placed it
and began to hammer home a hope.

The darkening sky, a black crow's cry
The stillness of a waiting world
Restrained my thudding wrist
Drew my eyes to a wooden pause

To a half-buried memory of you
To a sense of security turned sour
To a prison's perfect perimeter
To the futility of fences in the ninth hour.

As the first tears fell, the drops
That precede the storm,
I lowered my hammer, to ask
the origin, the outcome of my task.

A fence is a fence.
A defence.
A pretence.
An offence.

From whence came the sword
That pierced my heart, to turn
me from habit to honesty
To cut across the great divide.

To challenge me. To hide
or to hope. Neither wood
nor rope could hold
nor my foolish frame withhold.

So must I at the last nail
decide
In whose garden I stand and
how wide

the gap to be bridged between
fenced-in hopes and the hand
That beckons from the other
side.

MARY MOLLINEUX

It was in her mid-thirties, while in prison for attending Quaker meetings, that Mary Southworth met Henry Mollineux who had been convicted of the same offence. They married in 1685 in her home town of Warrington, Lancashire. When he was imprisoned again for non- payment of tithes, she appealed to Bishop Stratford and got him released. Fruits of Retirement, *or* Miscellaneous Poems Moral and Divine *was her only published collection.*

from To her Lord

Alas, how hard a thing
It is to bring
Into a true subjection flesh and blood,
Quietly to entertain
(And not complain)
Those exercises that attend for good!

My Life, my Joy, my Love,
If thus thou please to prove
And exercise my poor perplexed mind,
Teach me to wait in fear,
That I may learn to hear
What trials may attend, of any kind:

And, guarded by thy Ray,
Walk in the way,
That leads directly to the throne of grace;
Where in humility,
Poor I may be
Admitted to sit down i' th' heav'nly place.

And there to thee discharge
My griefs at large,
As to a Bosom-Friend, that bears with me,
And often passes by
Faults of infirmity:
Alas! I cannot bear too much for thee!

MARY HERBERT, COUNTESS OF PEMBROKE
1561–1621

Why did Sir Philip Sidney's famous romance Arcadia *first appear as 'The Countess of Pembroke's Arcadia'? The answer is that his sister Mary, for whose amusement the work was first written, revised and extended it greatly after his death. Mary, married to Henry Herbert, Earl of Pembroke, also worked with her brother on a metrical version of the Psalms, again much revised by her, and was the patroness of various contemporary poets. Yet her brother still receives credit for her work, and one of her poems was even attributed to Spenser!*

Psalm 13

How long, O Lord, shall I forgotten be?
    What? ever?
How long wilt thou thy hidden face from me
    Dissever?

How long shall I consult with carefull sprite[1]
    In anguish?
How long shall I with foes triumphant might
    Thus languish?

Behold me, Lord; let to thy hearing creep
    My crying;
Nay, give me eyes and light, lest that I sleep
    In dying:

Lest my foe brag, that in my ruin he
    Prevailed;
And at my fall they joy that, troublous, me
    Assailed.

No! no! I trust on thee, and joy in thy
    Great pity:
Still, therefore, of thy graces shall be my
    Song's ditty.

[1] Sprite = spirit

EMILY DICKINSON
1830–1886

I shall know why

I shall know why, when time is over,
And I have ceased to wonder why;
Christ will explain each separate anguish
In the fair schoolroom of the sky.

He will tell me what Peter promised,
And I, for wonder at his woe,
I shall forget the drop of anguish
That scalds me now, that scalds me now.

CHRISTINA ROSSETTI
1830–94

Uphill

Does the road wind uphill all the way?
    Yes, to the very end.
Will the day's journey take the whole long day?
    From morn to night, my friend.

But is there for the night a resting-place?
    A roof for when the slow, dark hours begin.
May not the darkness hide it from my face?
    You cannot miss that inn.

Shall I meet other wayfarers at night?
    Those who have gone before.
Then must I knock, or call when just in sight?
    They will not keep you waiting at that door.

Shall I find comfort, travel-sore and weak?
    Of labour you shall find the sum.
Will there be beds for me and all who seek?
    Yea, beds for all who come.

'MICHAEL FIELD'

(Katharine Bradley, 1846–1914 and Edith Cooper, 1842–1913)

Birmingham-born Katharine and her Kenilworth-born niece Edith lived together from the time when Katharine was sixteen and Edith four. Katharine, a tobacco manufacturer's daughter, studied at Cambridge, Paris and Bristol, educating her niece herself. Together they wrote twenty-seven tragedies and eight volumes of verse, including many poems based on the works of the Greek poet Sappho. In 1907 they both became Catholics. They died of cancer within a year of each other.

Aridity

O soul, canst thou not understand
Thou art not left alone,
As a dog to howl and moan
His master's absence? Thou art as a book
Left in a room that He forsook,
But returns to by and by,
A book of His dear choice,—
That quiet waiteth for His Hand,
That quiet waiteth for His Eye,
That quiet waiteth for His Voice.

MRS EDWARD DOWDEN
Nineteenth century

The only thing that seems to be known about the authorship of this poem is that it was by the wife of Edward Dowden (1843-1913), Irish critic and professor of English literature at Trinity College, Dublin. Dowden married twice. The poem is probably by his second wife, Elizabeth Dickinson (née West), who also edited his poems posthumously.

Adrift

Unto my faith as to a spar, I bring
   My love—and Faith and Love adrift I cast
   On a dim sea. I know not if at last
They the eternal shore of God shall find.

I know that neither waves nor wind
   Can sunder them, the cords are tied so fast
   That faith shall never—doubts and dangers past—
Come safe to land and Love be left behind.

GRACE RHYS
1865–1929

It was at a garden party given by W.B.Yeats that Irish country squire's daughter Grace Little met poet, editor and anthologist Ernest Rhys, whom she was later to marry. The marriage was happy and the couple had a son and two daughters. Little is known of Grace's poetic work.

The pavilions of peace

Within the circle of His peace
The Lord of life abides and is.

Out of His peace I cannot go,
Now that its still delight I know.

Clad in its beam I spend the day,
A poor weed dressed in a silver ray.

Earth's fields at evening mourn the light:
In His pavilions there is no night.

Peace holds the darkness, till it seems
His hand upon me in my dreams.

And when I wake, in light it falls,
A window in my chamber walls.

Dressed in His peace the hills arise,
And shine like towers of Paradise.

The green trees standing in the sun,
Are flames of His brightness every one.

Flowers, blown in a secret place,
In their day of beauty desire His face.

Lit by His thought, His children's eyes
Are lamps before His mysteries.

Within the peace of His great halls,
Where moon and star ingem the walls,

I have had gifts at His hand of light,
That make one treasure of day and night;

Chrism of the eyes, a seal on the mouth,
A harp at the ear set, a sun in the south.

Through His pavilions flows white peace,
The fountain of my felicities.

Out of His peace I may never go;
I should perish of thirst for that stream's white flow.

ANGELA MORGAN
Died 1957

Born in Washington DC and educated at Columbia and Chautauqua Universities, Angela wrote for the Chicago American *and other journals, and in 1936 was Poet Laureate of the US Federation of Women's Clubs. She spent three years in England, where her poetry was published in* The Spectator, *and gave readings across the United States. Her collected poems,* Rockets to the Sun, *appeared in 1957.*

Kinship

I am aware,
As I go commonly sweeping the stair,
Doing my part of the everyday care—
Human and simple my lot and share—
   I am aware of a marvellous thing:
   Voices that murmur and ethers that ring
   In the far stellar spaces where cherubim sing;
I am aware of the passion that pours
Down the channels of fire through Infinity's doors;
   Forces terrific, with melody shod,
   Music that mates with the pulses of God.
I am aware of the glory that runs
From the core of myself to the core of the suns,
   Bound to the stars by invisible chains,
   Blaze of eternity now in my veins,
   Seeing the rush of ethereal rains,
Here in the midst of the everyday air—
   I am aware.

I am aware,
As I sit quietly here in my chair,
Sewing or reading or braiding my hair—
Human and simple my lot and my share—
   I am aware of the systems that swing
   Through the aisles of creation on heavenly wing,
   I am aware of a marvellous thing,
Trail of the comets in furious flight,
Thunders of beauty that shatter the night,
   Terrible triumph of pageants that march
   To the trumpets of time through eternity's arch.

I am aware of the splendour that ties
All the things of the earth to the things of the skies,
  Here in my body the heavenly heat,
  Here in my flesh the melodious beat
  Of the planets that circle Divinity's feet.
As I silently sit here in my chair,
  I am aware.

FREDA CAVE
Born 1922

Freda lives in Wiltshire in England and has published poems mainly in poetry magazines, and in parish and diocesan magazines. This poem, which appeared in Christian Poetry 1976, takes an unusual 'angel's eye view' of reality.

Presence

Your solid bodies fill a little of the room,
two of you, lightly weaving words
on the loom of your time and space.

A blind-cord taps, the face of the younger
turns towards the window, smiling slightly:
Charlie again, she says. Charlie, the name
you use when inexplicable things happen—
a tap spurts, an untouched door clicks open.

It is not my name, but it is my self.

How, how to make you know that we are here?
uncountable millions of us, in a little space
that three of you would crowd:
not the space that is full of you and your existence—
but this you have no image for, not yet...

There—the other of you looks up startled:
I coincided somehow with your sense,
made you aware (or was it someone else?) of us here:

the presence and presentness of Eternity
crowding the vast emptinesses of your air.

CIA CHESTER
Contemporary

A friend and protégée of the agnostic American poet Anne Sexton, Cia Chester became a Christian after Sexton's suicide. Two of her unusual, penetrating poems, including this one, have appeared in Fellowship of Christian Writers' poetry anthologies, but no further information seems to be available.

And then the shattering of images...

I learned to worship in cliches,
caught myself talking to the god who made all
polite things;
sun in the left-hand corner of the sky
& the shade o'green which goes cheery
in nice people's home, like daisy.

& then Kate was gone blind
& I lying on my grandmother's warm pink couch
& then Kate's unconscious

(I was only in her house once
but I smelled death then,
her parents lived in the dark.
they were rich so I forgot to worry.)

& now she's dying
& the whole family
all there exposed in that
hospital, naked
thoughts pound unembarrassed

*

I want to be in   on their healing.
my thinking is moving quiet child, hurt
& there no apologies. I sense God's thinking my speed
right now with a part of his love

& wanting to be an extension of Jesus' hand
I touch the window (behind the couch
which holds me warm)
my whole self is stopped, sensitive to her dying; I feel
the molecules in the glass tremble.

I say, God is it okay? my fingertips on this glass

can be you touching her body   in Boston (?)

*

if this is Him & I be a child in feeling
the way he feels it through and through then
prayer's changed for me now.
I think—
no more sweet little blessings,
gotta take each one onto the insides like
Kate & touch my fingertips gentle
over them & learn their whimpering out.

I be a blind potter meeting tender each new
texture glaze.
I be clay in the Potter's hand
yielding.

18 Praise

MARY HERBERT
1561–1621

*'Visual games' like this acrostic (where the first letter of each line makes a phrase)
were a favourite feature of seventeenth-century poetry. Allowance must be made in this
one for contemporary spelling!*

Psalm 117: Laudate Dominum

Praise him that aye
Remains the same:
All tongues display
Iehova's fame.
Sing all that share
This earthly ball,
His mercies are
Expos'd to all:
Like as the word
Once he doth give,
Roll'd in record,
Doth time outlive.

ELIZABETH ROWE
1674–1737

Encouraged by her father, a well-off Somerset cloth merchant and former dissenting minister, Elizabeth Singer began writing verse at twelve. For her first anthology, under the name of Philomela, she was hailed as a champion for women against 'the tyranny of the prouder sex'. She was courted by the poet Matthew Prior, but she rejected him for his flippancy and drinking. At thirty-six she married twenty-three-year-old scholar Thomas Rowe, who died of tuberculosis five years later. She inherited substantial property from her father but gave half her income to charity each year. Her Devout Exercises of the Heart were edited after her death by Isaac Watts who, in a dedicatory verse, wrote: 'I was all ears, and Philomela's song Was all divine delight.'

Hymn

The glorious armies of the sky
  To thee, Almighty King,
Triumphant anthems consecrate,
  And hallelujahs sing.

But still their most exalted flights
  Fall vastly short of thee:
How distant then must human praise
  From thy perfections be!

Yet how, my God, shall I refrain
  When to my ravished sense
Each creature everywhere around
  Displays thy excellence!

The active lights that shine above,
  In their eternal dance,
Reveal their skilful Maker's praise
  With silent elegance.

The blushes of the morn confess
  That thou art still more fair,
When in the East its beams revive,
  To gild the fields of air.

The fragrant, the refreshing breeze
  Of ev'ry flow'ry bloom
In balmy whispers own, from thee
  Their pleasing odours come.

The singing birds, the warbling winds,
    And waters murm'ring fall
To praise the first Almighty Cause
    With diff'rent voices call.

Thy num'rous works exalt thee thus,
    And shall I silent be?
No; rather let me cease to breathe,
    Than cease from praising thee!

MARGUERITE WILKINSON

1883–1928

Canadian-born Marguerite Bigelow grew up in the United States, a sensitive, frail child with 'a passionate love for the outdoors'. She began to write while studying English at North-Western University. In 1919 she married James Wilkinson, principal of Roosevelt School, New York, and enjoyed a domestic life with annual camping and trout-fishing trips. She reviewed poetry, lectured and wrote on new poets, and had a keen interest in Christian mysticism. After a breakdown she learned to fly to conquer fear. She swam in the sea every morning and went flying every afternoon. She was drowned practising swimming stunts at the age of forty-four.

A chant out of doors

God of grave nights,
God of brave mornings,
God of silent noon,
Hear my salutation!
   For where the rapids rage white and scornful
   I have passed safely, filled with wonder;
   Where the sweet pools dream under willows
   I have been swimming, filled with joy.

God of round hills,
God of green valleys,
God of clear springs,
Hear my salutation!
   For where the moose feeds I have eaten berries,
   Where the moose drinks I have drunk deep;
   And under clear skies I have known love.

God of great trees,
God of wild grasses,
God of little flowers,
Hear my salutation!
   For where the deer crops and the beaver plunges
   Near the river I have pitched my tent;
   Where the pines cast aromatic needles
   On the still flowers I have known peace.

God of grave nights,
God of brave mornings,
God of silent noon,
Hear my salutation.

VERONICA ZUNDEL
Born 1953

Song

I scan you on the figured page
in tales of every distant age
and chant you in a holy song
but yet I hear, I see you wrong

I am so small
you are so all

and I would scent you in a flower
that flares and fails from hour to hour
and count your liberality
in berries bright upon the tree

but they are small
and you are all

or might I feel you in the sky
your cloudwind lifts my soul so high
or might I taste you in the spring
new-risen, cleanly carolling

I am so small
you are so all

but narrow is my inward sight
I do not spell your meanings right
and guttering my outward gaze
I do not steady trace your ways

my steps are small
to map your all

then break me wide your raging word
in flintstruck light from darkness stirred
and break me wide your dancing love
that soars the hawk, that swoops the dove

I am so small
you are so all in all

Acknowledgments

We are grateful to the copyright holders for permission to include the poems listed below.

Freda Cave, 'Presence' from *Christian Poetry 1976*, reprinted by permission of the author.

Gwen Clear, 'The goodwife relents', from *The Eldest Sister*, published by Longmans, 1927.

Frances Cornford, 'All Souls' night', from *Collected Poems*, Cresset Press, reprinted by permission of the publisher.

Joy Davidman, 'Snow in Madrid', from *Letter to a Comrade*, Yale University Press, reprinted by permission of the publisher.

Lesley Dickens, 'The Fence', from *Christian Poetry 1989*, reprinted by permission of the author.

Barbara Dickinson, 'Go to the ant', from *Christian Poetry 1979*, reprinted by permission of the author.

Rosemary Dobson, 'Cock crow', from *Selected Poems*, Collins/Angus & Robertson Publishers, reprinted by permission of the publisher.

Madeleine L'Engle, 'O Sapientia', from *A Widening Light*, Harold Shaw Publishers, reprinted by permission of the publisher.

U.A.Fanthorpe, 'The list', from *Selected Poems*, Peterloo Poets and Penguin Books, reprinted by permission of the publisher.

Elizabeth Jennings, 'In a garden', from *Growing Points*, Carcanet, reprinted by permission of the publisher.

Janet Lewis, 'A lullaby', from *Poems Old and New 1918–1978*, Swallow Press/Ohio University Press, reprinted by permission of the author and publisher.

Phyllis McGinley, 'First lesson from A girl's-eye view of relatives', 'A garland of precepts', from *Times Three*, Sheed and Ward Limited, reprinted by permission of the publisher.

Elma Mitchell, 'The corset', from *People Etcetera*, Peterloo Poets, reprinted by permission of the publisher.

Moira O'Neill, 'Her sister', from *Collected Poems*, Blackwood, reprinted by permission of the publisher.

Evangeline Paterson, 'Variations on a street song', 'Civilisation', from *Bringing the Water Hyacinth to Africa*, Taxus Press, 1983, reprinted by permission of the publisher. 'A wish for my children', from *Lucifer at the Fair*, Taxus Press, 1991, reproduced by permission of the author.

Marion Pitman, 'Hero', from *Lunch with Veronica*, Eating People Publications, 1988; 'Polly' and 'Easter Midnight Service' from *Heart to Heart*, Arts Centre Group, 1979, reprinted by permission of the author.

Ruth Pitter, 'The Irish patriarch', from *Poems 1926–1966*, Cresset Press, reprinted by permission of the publisher.

Kathleen Raine, 'Exile', first published by Hamish Hamilton, reprinted by permission of the publisher.

Irina Ratushinskaya, 'Spider-mathematician', from *No, I'm Not Afraid*, translated by David McDuff, Bloodaxe Books, reprinted by permission of the publisher.

Anne Ridler, 'Villanelle for the middle of the way', from *New and Selected Poems*, Faber and Faber Ltd, reprinted by permission of the publisher.

Elizabeth Rooney, 'Creator' from *A Widening Light*, Harold Shaw Publishers, reprinted by permission of the author.

Luci Shaw, 'Circles', from *Polishing the Petoskey Stone*, Harold Shaw Publishers, reprinted by permission of the publisher.

Stevie Smith, 'What is she writing?', from *The Collected Poems of Stevie Smith*, Penguin 20th Century Classics (London) and New Directions Publishing Corporation (New York), reprinted by permission of the publishers.

Pauline Stainer, 'The catalyst', from *The Honeycomb*, Bloodaxe Books, reprinted by permission of the publisher.

Teresa of Avila, 'Hymn for the nuns' new habits', from *The Complete Works of St Teresa*, translated by E. Allison Peers, reprinted by permission of the publisher.

Patience Tuckwell, 'Enigma' from *Twenty-Four Poems*, 1974, reprinted by permission of the author.

Judith Wright, 'Woman to man', from *Collected Poems*, Collins/Angus & Robertson Publishers, reprinted by permission of the publisher.

Every effort has been made to trace and contact copyright holders. If there are any inadvertent omissions in the acknowledgments we apologize to those concerned.